SLAVERY IN AMERICAN HISTORY

ABOLITIONISTS AND SLAVE RESISTANCE

BREAKING THE CHAINS OF SLAVERY

JUDITH EDWARDS

FOREWORD BY DR. HENRY LOUIS GATES, JR.

Enslow Publishers, Inc.

40 Industrial Road	PO Box 38
Box 398	Aldershot
Berkeley Heights, NJ 07922	Hants GU12 6BP
USA	UK

http://www.enslow.com

Library of Congress Cataloging-in-Publication Data

Edwards, Judith.
    Abolitionists and slave resistance: breaking the chains of slavery /Judith Edwards.
       v. cm.— (Slavery in American history)
    Includes bibliographical references and index.
    Contents: Events leading to abolition—Slavery and the Revolutionary War—The anti-slavery movement gathers force—Abolitionists organize—The Amistad and the new decade—The rebels and the runaways—Escape from slavery and fugitive slave laws—Leading to war—On the anti-slavery side—From slave to soldier.
    ISBN 0-7660-2155-6
    1. Antislavery movements—United States—History—Juvenile literature.
2. Abolitionists—United States—History—Juvenile literature. 3. Slave insurrections—United States—History—Juvenile literature. [1. Antislavery movements. 2. Abolitionists. 3. Slave insurrections. 4. United States—History—Civil War, 1861–1865.] I. Title. II. Series.
E441.E34   2004
326'.8'0973—dc22

                                         2003013457

Printed in the United States of America

10 9 8 7 6 5 4 3 2 1

To Our Readers: We have done our best to make sure all Internet Addresses in this book were active and appropriate when we went to press. However, the author and the publisher have no control over and assume no liability for the material available on those Internet sites or on other Web sites they may link to. Any comments or suggestions can be sent by e-mail to comments@enslow.com or to the address on the back cover.

Illustration Credits: © The Art Archive, p. 76; Charles Hogarth, *Ready-To-Use Illustrations of American Landmarks*, Mineola, N.Y.: Dover Publications, Inc. 1998, pp. 45, 81; © ClipArt.com, p. 7; Courtesy Library of Congress, reproduced from the *Dictionary of American Portraits*, published by Dover Publications, Inc., in 1967, p. 72; Courtesy Library of Congress, Brady-Handy Collection, reproduced from the *Dictionary of American Portraits*, published by Dover Publications, Inc., in 1967, pp. 1 (left), 40; Culver Pictures, p. 21; Engraved by Richard W. Dodson after a painting by Thomas Scully, reproduced from the *Dictionary of American Portraits*, published by Dover Publications, Inc., in 1967, p. 17; Enslow Publishers, Inc., pp. 69, 79; © Hemera Technologies, Inc., p. 56; Hulton Archive/Getty Images, pp. 41, 46; © Jane Reed, Harvard News Office, p. 5; Mary Evans Picture Library, p. 67; National Archives and Records Administration, pp. 3, 75, 97; New Haven Colonial Historical Society, p. 52; © North Wind Picture Archives, p. 74; Reproduced from the Collections of the Library of Congress, pp. 8–9, 31, 42, 54, 65, 82, 88, 90, 103, 104, 106; Reproduced from the *Dictionary of American Portraits*, published by Dover Publications, Inc., in 1967, pp. 1 (right), 34, 58.

Cover Illustration: National Archives and Records Administration (cover photo); reproduced from the Collections of the Library of Congress (cover background).

⇾ C O N T E N T S ⇽

American Slavery's Undying Legacy

While the Thirteenth Amendment outlawed slavery in the United States in 1865, the impact of that institution continued to be felt long afterward, and in many ways is still being felt today. The broad variety of experiences encompassed within that epoch of American history can be difficult to encapsulate. Enslaved, free, owner, trader, abolitionist: each "category" hides a complexity of experience as varied as the number of individuals who occupied these identities.

One thing is certain: in spite of how slavery has sometimes been portrayed, very few, if any, enslaved blacks were utter victims who quietly and passively accepted such circumstances. Those who claimed ownership over Africans and African Americans used violence, intimidation, and other means to wield a great degree of power and control. But as human beings—and as laborers within an economic system that depended on labor—all enslaved blacks retained varying degrees of agency within that system.

The "Slavery in American History" series provides a strong and needed overview of the most important aspects of American slavery, from the first transport of African slaves to the American colonies, to the long fight for abolition, to the lasting impact of slavery on America's economy, politics, and culture. Only by understanding American slavery and its complex legacies can we begin to understand the challenge facing not just African Americans, but all Americans: To make certain that our country is a living and breathing embodiment of the principles enunciated in the Constitution of the United States. Only by understanding the past can we mend the present and ensure the rights of our future generations.

—**Henry Louis Gates, Jr.,** *Ph.D., W.E.B. Du Bois Professor of the Humanities, Chair of the Department African and African-American Studies, Director of the W.E.B. Du Bois Institute for African and African-American Research, Harvard University.*

Dr. Henry Louis Gates, Jr., Series Advisor

Dr. Henry Louis Gates, Jr., is author the of a number of books including: *The Trials of Phillis Wheatley: America's First Poet and Her Encounters with the Founding Fathers*, *The African-American Century* (with Cornel West), *Little Known Black History Facts*, *Africana: The Encyclopedia of the African American Experience*, *Wonders of the African World*, *The Future of The Race* (with Cornel West), *Colored People: A Memoir*, *Loose Cannons: Notes on the Culture Wars*, *The Signifying Monkey: Towards A Theory of Afro-American Literary Criticism*, *Figures in Black: Words, Signs, and the Racial Self*, and *Thirteen Ways of Looking at a Black Man*.

Professor Gates earned his M.A. and Ph.D. in English Literature from Clare College at the University of Cambridge. Before beginning his work at Harvard in 1991, he taught at Yale, Cornell, and Duke universities. He has been named one of *Time* magazine's "25 Most Influential Americans," received a National Humanities Medal, and was elected to the American Academy of Arts and Letters.

❖ I N T R O D U C T I O N ❖

Slavery in the United States was abolished, forever, on December 6, 1865—the day the Thirteenth Amendment to the Constitution took effect.

Almost two centuries earlier, in February of 1688, a group of Quakers in Germantown, Pennsylvania, wrote down the first documented protest against slavery in what would one day become the United States. The wording left no doubt about what those Quakers thought of slavery:

> These are the reasons why we are against the traffic of mensbody. . . . Is there any that would be done or handled at this manner . . . to be sold or made a slave for all the time of this life?. . . . [H]ave these Negroes not as much right to fight for their freedom as you have to keep them slaves?[1]

Wherever slavery exists, of course, rebellion against its terrible loss of individual freedom also exists. Between 1619 and 1865, there were at least two hundred fifty revolts and conspiracies by slaves in the North American British Colonies and, later, in the United States.[2] Both slaves and free black men resisted slavery. They argued against slavery, wrote and spoke publicly about the injustices of slavery, and led or supported rebellions against slavery.

What happened in the nearly two hundred years between a Quaker declaration that cries out against slavery,

In addition to slavery, Quakers were also against violence and war. Here, some Quakers take part in a prayer meeting.

and the actual *ending* of the institution? Abolitionists, both black and white, campaigned to end slavery in the first half of the nineteenth century. The Germantown Protest can be seen as a precursor of the abolitionist movement. The Quakers' protest asserts that the enslaved have a right to be free.

Though abolitionists and slave resisters varied in their beliefs and acted in different ways, they all worked against slavery. So, why did it take so long to end an institution that was so much the opposite of the ideals of freedom, self-determination, and equality expressed in the United States Declaration of Independence?

1

RESISTANCE TO SLAVERY BEFORE THE REVOLUTION

ABRAHAM LINCOLN LIKED TO EMPHASIZE points in his speeches with little stories, called anecdotes. In 1860, he illustrated a speech about slavery with an anecdote about an argument between two ministers. "Do you see that word?" said one minister, pointing to a word in the Bible. "Of course I do!" said the other minister. Then the first minister put a large gold coin over the word, saying, "Do you see it now?"

President Lincoln's story was a warning about the economic stranglehold of slavery, and how difficult it was for people to see what was right and moral when so much money was at stake. "Whether the owners of this species of property [slaves] do really see it as it is," Lincoln continued, "it is not for me to say, but if they do, they see it as it is through 2,000,000,000 [two billion] of dollars, and that is a pretty thick coating. . . . they do not see it as we see it. . . . this immense pecuniary [financial] interest has its influence upon their minds."[1]

It was not only slaveholders in the South who based their entire way of life and financial security around slavery. Northerners who engaged in trade and business dealings with these slaveholders also were diverted from human rights by economic habits that became economic necessities. The way of life that allowed and embraced slavery took several centuries to harden. As it did, many forms of protest by slaves besides outright rebellions developed.

"Indentured Servants" in the 1600s

Formal bondage of Africans was first introduced to the colonies in 1619 at Jamestown, Virginia. A Dutch ship, arriving on the shores of the James River, traded its cargo of twenty Africans for food. Modern historians cannot agree as to whether these Africans were slaves or indentured servants.

Indentured servitude was one of the main forms of hired labor in the early 1600s. Indentured servants, who could be white or black, were people who had agreed to work for a specified number of years (usually five or seven) in return for transportation, room, board, and employment. After the term had been served, the servant was granted freedom. Although indentured servants were often treated much like slaves, their legal status was very different—they had many more rights. As economic conditions in

England and Europe improved during the later seventeenth century, white indentured servitude gradually disappeared from the colonies. Planters, who needed a dependable supply of labor for their "cash crops," tobacco and rice, increasingly relied on Africans.

It is hard to trace exactly when race became a factor in enslavement. However, by the 1640s, legal decisions (especially in the tobacco-growing colonies, such as Virginia and North Carolina) reflected different standards for Africans than for white colonists. Courts began to accept the notion of lifetime bondage for African Americans. In the 1660s, Virginia decreed that a child would follow the condition of the mother, thus making lifetime servitude inheritable in that colony.[2] By 1665, slavery was fully accepted in much of what would become the United States.

Slavery, of course, did not begin in North America. Ancient Greece, ancient Egypt, central Africa, and China all had slavery. Enslavement of Africans was already established in the Caribbean, Mexico, and Central and South America before it became customary in the North American British colonies.

Rebellion is also part of the long historical record of slavery. In addition to the more than two hundred fifty slave rebellions and conspiracies in British North America between 1619 and 1865, there were also "at least one hundred fifty-five documented mutinies" aboard slave ships, according to naval historian W. Jeffrey Bolster.[3]

Early Slave Rebellions

The earliest recorded slave revolts in the Western Hemisphere were on the Caribbean islands, where slavery was adopted even before the North American colonies were settled. There were rebellions in Hispaniola in 1522, Puerto Rico in 1527, New Spain [Mexico] in 1537, and Honduras in 1548.[4]

Rebellions against slavery in the British North American colonies were recorded as early as 1663. In that year, an organized group of slaves and hired servants in Gloucester County, Virginia, escaped to the woods. This was one of the key events that contributed to stricter laws that defined white "servants" differently from black "slaves." Although both black slaves and white indentured servants often ran away, "because of their color, slaves found it more difficult than servants to escape. . . . blacks were presumed to be slaves unless they could show otherwise," writes historian Peter Kolchin. "Racial distinction, in short, facilitated enslavement."[5]

In New York in 1712, twenty-three slaves revolted, setting fire to buildings and then killing at least nine white people and injuring several others. Others joined them before militia units and soldiers stationed nearby responded. Some rebels were killed, and twenty-seven were captured, all of whom committed suicide or were executed.

A revolt in Stono, South Carolina, in 1739 was led by an Angolan slave named Jemmy or Tommy. He used drums—a traditional form of communication in Africa—to call together about twenty men and women on a Sunday morning. The drums helped to gather as many as a hundred more recruits, as the slaves marched twelve miles. They killed several families and looted the colonists' farms along the way. (One family known for its kindness toward slaves was spared.) The revolt ended when the rebels stopped in the afternoon to celebrate their victory and were caught by a hastily assembled militia. Many were killed. Others escaped, but were captured and executed over the next several days. One group that stayed together was caught and defeated a week later, thirty miles away. One leader of the rebellion hid in the woods for three years and was only captured when two other runaway slaves betrayed him, hoping to earn favor for themselves.[6]

Again in New York in 1741, several fires—thought to be the result of arson by slaves—created public panic and hysteria. Historians are not clear whether slaves were actually involved in the arson in New York. It is clear, however, that in the widespread frenzy almost one hundred slaves were hanged, burned at the stake, or exiled in a "witch hunt" that continued for several weeks.[7]

Other Forms of Resistance

Other, more personal, forms of resistance are also part of the historical record. Murder, assault, arson, and poisonings by enslaved Africans, although not common, were noted regularly. In fact, says historian Peter Wood, white planters in South Carolina became so fearful about poisonings that, in 1751, the legislature in South Carolina passed "a law [that] forbade any slave [to] teach or instruct another slave in the knowledge of any poisonous root, plant, herb, or other poison whatever."[8]

Runaway slaves were also a constant annoyance to slaveholders, especially in the South. As early as 1739, several months before the Stono Rebellion, the South Carolina Assembly formed a committee to consider the problem of desertion by slaves. St. Augustine, a Spanish colonial settlement in Florida, had become a center for the trade in kidnapped or captured runaway slaves. The British and Spanish governments and their local representatives in North America often argued over this.

Partly to annoy the British, the King of Spain had, in 1733, proclaimed "liberty to Negro fugitives reaching St. Augustine [Florida] from the English colonies." All runaway slaves had to do was to accept baptism as Catholics and swear loyalty to the Spanish king. The decree was hardly enforced at all for a few years, but in 1738, a group of runaway slaves who had reached St. Augustine claimed their liberty. As a result, they were settled on land near St. Augustine, in the town of *Pueblo de Gracia Real de Santa Terese de Mose*. This town, under the much shorter nickname of "Moosa," became an almost mythical destination for escape-minded slaves in the American South.[9]

The slave revolts in other countries and the early revolts both north and south occurred before there was an organized antislavery movement that could be labeled as "abolitionist." The word *abolition* means "to abolish," or do away with. Throughout the 1700s, many individuals, especially Quakers—whose strong religious beliefs in individual liberty, dignity, and responsibility made them think of slavery as morally indefensible—took increasingly strong stands against slavery.

Samuel Sewall's *The Selling of Joseph*

Samuel Sewall, a merchant, judge, magistrate, and church deacon, wrote an influential pamphlet called "The Selling of Joseph," published in Boston in 1700. His public appeal

SOURCE DOCUMENT

It is likewise most lamentable to think, how in taking Negros out of Africa, and selling of them here, That which GOD has joined together men to boldly rend asunder; Men from their Country, Husbands from their Wives, Parents from their Children. How horrible is the Uncleanness, Mortality, if not Murder, that the Ships are guilty of that bring great Crouds of these miserable Men, and Women.[10]

In "The Selling of Joseph," Samuel Sewall made a religious argument against slavery.

spoke against the growing number of slaves in Puritan New England. Reprinted many times, his pamphlet said, "It is most certain that all Men, as they are the Sons of Adam, are, and have equal Right unto Liberty, and all other outward Comforts of Life."[11] His words inspired other antislavery advocates.

The first formal antislavery organization began in Philadelphia in 1775, and it had a very long name: "The Pennsylvania Society for Promoting the Abolition of Slavery, for the Relief of Free Negroes Unlawfully Held in Bondage, and for Improving the Condition of the African Race." (It was more commonly called the Pennsylvania Anti-Slavery Society.) After the Revolutionary War, its members included Benjamin Rush, a signer of the Declaration of Independence, and Benjamin Franklin, who became its president in 1789.

The northern colonies began to abolish slavery without a violent struggle as early as 1777. Some were influenced by Quakers such as John Woolman, who tried to persuade other Quakers to give up their own slaves. He used personal persuasion and a series of pamphlets to accomplish this.

Another influential Quaker, Benjamin Lay, was often caricatured in the press for both his violent temper and his very small stature. (He was 4 feet, 7 inches tall.) He published a book in 1737 that said on the title page: "All Slave-keepers, that keep the innocent in bondage, APOSTATES!" (An "apostate" is a traitor to one's religion.)

Benjamin Rush was a famous colonial doctor and patriot before he joined the antislavery cause.

According to one story, he once kidnapped the son of a slave-holding Quaker family and held him overnight, to force the parents to experience—as slave families did—the pain of losing a child.[12]

Thomas Jefferson, who was himself a slaveholder, put a section into an early draft of the Declaration of Independence denouncing slavery. Political pressure—from slaveholders in the South and from northern merchants who also benefited from the fruits of slavery—caused Jefferson's words to be deleted before the Declaration's adoption in 1776. Although he continued to be a slaveholder all his life, Jefferson once wrote in his *Notes on Virginia* that slavery ". . . must doubtless be an unhappy influence on the manners of our people . . . the most unremitting despotism on the one part, and degrading submissions on the other." He worried about its effect on children, both slave and free.[13]

By the time the Revolutionary War began in 1776, there was considerable antislavery sentiment in the northern states. Black participation in the war and the war itself would lead to active abolitionism.

2

SLAVERY AND THE
REVOLUTIONARY WAR

THE AMERICAN REVOLUTIONARY WAR WAS THE catalyst, or changing force, that led to emancipation for slaves in the northern states.

The first known African American to die by a British gun in events leading up to the Revolutionary War was Crispus Attucks, a runaway slave and a sailor. On March 5, 1770, a British soldier refused to pay a Boston barber for a haircut; the barber chased him down the street, and a jeering crowd gathered. The crowd included a group of sailors, and one of them was the tall and tough Crispus Attucks. A few nights earlier, some British soldiers had gotten into a fight with the locals, and everyone was on edge. More soldiers appeared, the jeering increased, and someone swung a stick at British Captain Thomas Preston. In the scuffle, Attucks tried to grab a soldier's rifle, but the soldier recovered it and shot him point-blank (so close that it is impossible to miss).

There was panic and more shooting. Attucks and four others lay dead.

This event came to be called the Boston Massacre by the colonial patriots. Attucks might not be remembered today except for the fact that at the British soldiers' trial, he was portrayed in the newspapers as a strong, determined, heroic attacker. "The irony of his heroism," writes historian Michael Lee Lanning, "was that as a black man, Crispus Attucks would not have enjoyed the benefits of American independence had he lived," meaning that African Americans enjoyed only very limited gains after the Revolution.[1]

When the Revolution began in 1776, the Continental Congress at first agreed to enlist slaves in the rebellion. Some free African-American men were already members of local militias. Both free African Americans and slaves distinguished themselves at the first major battles, the Battle of Lexington and Concord and the Battle of Bunker Hill. Because of his deeds at Bunker Hill, former slave Salem Poor was recommended by his superior officers for a special citation by the Massachusetts General Court. Peter Salem, a slave whose owner freed him so he could join the Minuteman militia, fought at Concord and at Bunker Hill. He shot and killed a British commander at Bunker Hill.

African-American Soldiers in the Revolutionary War
Although African-American soldiers were at first welcomed into the Revolutionary forces, slaves were not offered the

Peter Salem shot and killed Major Pitcairn, who had commanded the British troops at Lexington, Massachusetts.

incentive of freedom for joining the fight. General George Washington, a slave owner himself, soon became uneasy at the presence of numbers of armed African Americans. Shortly after the first major battles, the Continental Army began to exclude black soldiers, although some state militias continued to accept them.

To take advantage of the anger this decision caused among African Americans, Virginia's Royal Governor, Lord Dunmore, issued a proclamation in November 1775 promising freedom to any slave owned by a Patriot master who joined the Loyalist (supporting the British) forces.

(Runaway slaves belonging to Loyalists were returned to their masters.) Within a month, three hundred African-American men had joined Lord Dunmore's "Ethiopian Regiment." Because the battle quickly moved away from Virginia to other areas, probably no more than eight hundred slaves succeeded in actually joining Dunmore's regiment. An estimated thirty thousand runaways, however, were inspired to support or follow the British throughout the war.[2]

As the war raged on through 1777, the Continental Army again changed its mind. "Quietly reversing its policy, the Continental command accepted all Negroes sent by the states. The recruiting of Negroes was further stimulated by the system of substitution, through which a draftee could avoid service by producing someone else to take his place," write historians Leon Fishel and Benjamin Quarles. Often a slave would be sent as a substitute for the master.[3] African-American recruits were again welcomed. Now the reward for serving in the military was freedom, and in some states a land bounty.

When the British Army invaded Georgia in 1788, the Continental Congress began to consider several proposals that would emancipate and arm thousands of slaves in Georgia and South Carolina. However, all such proposals were rejected by those two states. As New Hampshire delegate William Whipple put it in a letter, the southern states rejected those proposals because they "would lay a foundation for the Abolition of Slavery in America."[4]

Caesar "Tarrant" and James "Armistead"

African Americans were active on sea as well as on land. Many blacks, both free men and slaves, were engaged as pilots in the state navies in the South. Virginia employed many African-American pilots who knew the waterways around Chesapeake Bay. One outstanding African-American pilot was Caesar, a slave belonging to Carter Tarrant of Hampton. For his part in the capture of the British ship *Fanny* by the schooner *Patriot*, Caesar earned his freedom.

Another celebrated combatant in the Revolution was James, the slave of Virginian William Armistead. With Armistead's permission, James enlisted with the Marquis de Lafayette, the Frenchman who became a famous American Revolutionary commander. James became his most trusted spy. In 1786, on Lafayette's recommendation, the Virginia legislature bought James his freedom.

In all, about five thousand African-American men were enlisted in the new American army as soldiers or as military laborers. According to historians Fischel and Quarles, two thousand of those numbers served in the Navy, "naval authorities being much more receptive to Negroes than were their military counterparts."[5] The British recruited heavily, and runaway slaves helped the British cause on land, at sea, and as military laborers. "At the war's end, most of the Negroes who had served with the British sailed away with them—four thousand from Savannah, six thousand from Charleston, and four thousand from New York."[6]

Before the American Revolution, nearly every African

This is to certify that the bearer by the name of James has done essential services to me while I had the honour to command in this state. His intelligences from the enemy's camp were industriously collected and faithfully delivered. He perfectly acquitted himself with some important commissions I gave him and appears to me entitled to every reward his situation can admit of. Done under my hand, Richmond, November 21st, 1784.

Lafayette[7]

Marquis de Lafayette wrote this recommendation for his slave, James, after the Revolutionary War.

American throughout the British North American colonies was a slave. By the war's end, almost sixty thousand of those slaves had won, earned, or claimed their freedom, and many of them headed for the cities. As historian W. Jeffrey Bolster writes, "Ultimately, the presence of runaways in capitols such as London, Boston, and Philadelphia fueled the embryonic antislavery movement."[8]

3

THE NEW NATION

C LEARLY, THE WAR PROVIDED OPPORTUNITIES for many African-American men and women in the colonies to change their status. These changes, in turn, spurred religious and humanitarian efforts to end slavery.

In 1777, Vermont declared itself an independent "commonwealth," and became the first United States territory to abolish slavery. While it did not become a state until 1781, it was, says historian William Miller, "proud also to be the first never to have had slavery within its boundaries."[1]

After the Revolution, Massachusetts in 1780 and New Hampshire in 1783 enacted absolute prohibitions against slavery. All the other states that freed their slaves did so only "gradually." In Pennsylvania, all African Americans born in the state after March 1, 1780, would become free at age twenty-eight. In Rhode Island, African Americans born after March 1784 were free. Connecticut enacted gradual emancipation in 1784, New York in 1799, and New Jersey in 1804.

The Constitution of the Commonwealth of Pennsylvania was drafted in 1776 and officially adopted when Pennsylvania became a state in 1780. Because of antislavery sentiment in Quaker Pennsylvania, the constitution took its language almost directly from the Declaration of Independence. The Pennsylvania document stated: "That all men are born equally free and independent, and have certain natural, inherent and inalienable rights, amongst which are, the enjoying and defending life and liberty, acquiring, possessing and protecting property, and pursuing and obtaining happiness and safety."[2] Despite these ideals, however, the "gradual emancipation" law did not actually free a single slave living in Pennsylvania. Seven thousand black people remained slaves even after it was passed.[3]

Prominent men such as Benjamin Franklin, Benjamin Rush, and the Marquis de Lafayette raised their voices in protest against slavery. Other religious groups—Methodists, Unitarians, Presbyterians, Baptists, and Congregationalists—joined with the Quakers in helping both free and enslaved blacks, and in advocating an end to slavery.

Slaves in the South had taken advantage of the confusion, disorder, and absence of authority during the war. They had run away. Because the slaveholders' economic well-being was tied to slave labor, the growing antislavery sentiment in the North caused them to become heavily resistant to reform. For southern plantation owners, slavery was an industry.[4] Long before abolitionist fervor took hold around 1830 in white New England, African-American antislavery activists traded on the post-Revolutionary movement to remove "the last traces of slavery in the North and to call for its abolition in the South."[5]

In 1797, four escaped slaves from North Carolina asked Congress to consider the question of slavery. A group of free African Americans living in Philadelphia appealed to Congress in 1800 to look at African trade and fugitive slave laws, and consider gradual emancipation of all African-American slaves. Three years later, another group of free African Americans living in Philadelphia petitioned Congress in the same cause. None of the petitions was so much as considered for debate.

Ideas of Freedom Take Hold

The years 1790 to 1810, were marked by enormous complexity about issues of equality, slavery, and race. The ideals of the Declaration of Independence, the practical effects of the Revolutionary War, and a successful slave revolt on the Caribbean island of Saint-Domingue all excited African-American hopes and aspirations. As historian Sylvia Frey puts it, "Blacks, slave and free, urban and rural, artisan and field hand, literate and illiterate, were swept up by the force of ideological energy."[6]

Two facts will illustrate the confusion and complexity of those years. Despite emancipation laws, according to Ira Berlin, "in 1810, there were still some 27,000 slaves in [the] so-called free states."[7] In the South, Berlin notes, "during

SOURCE DOCUMENT

The unhappy man who has long been treated as a brute Animal too frequently sinks beneath the common standard of the human species; the galling chains that bind his body, do also fetter his intellectual faculties, and impair the social affections of his heart; accustomed to move like a meer Machine by the will of a master, Reflection is suspended; he has not the power of Choice, and Reason and Conscience have but little influence over his conduct, because he is chiefly governed by the passion of Fear. He is poor & friendless, perhaps worn out by extreme Labour Age and Disease. Under such circumstances Freedom may often prove a misfortune to himself and prejudicial to Society.[8]

Although the Pennsylvania Society for the Abolition of Slavery was an antislavery organization, its "Address to the Public" inferred that blacks were inferior to whites because of the way they had been treated as slaves. However, contrary to what the above excerpt states, African Americans rose above the harsh conditions of slavery and were still able to reason, make important choices, and resist slave owners.

the early years of the nineteenth century, almost one-third of Charleston's free black families joined the slaveholders' ranks" by becoming owners of slaves themselves.[9]

While most of the northern states enacted some form of emancipation, however gradual, African-American people in the North still struggled for their freedoms. Free African Americans were often subjected to restrictions hardly different from those imposed on slaves: They could not vote or testify in court, and they had to observe curfews and travel restrictions. Many slave owners freed their slaves legally, but forced them to agree to indentured servitude instead. Still other northern slave owners took advantage of gradual abolition laws by simply selling their slaves in the South before the laws demanded they free them.

Although the southern states remained committed to slavery, slaves were more than ever committed to freedom. As Berlin says, "slaves—who had greatly expanded their independence in their owners' absence—did not willingly surrender their wartime gains."[10] The successful slave revolt in Saint-Domingue that began in 1789 and resulted in the creation of the Republic of Haiti inspired both slaves and free African Americans with dreams of true liberty.

Revolution in Saint-Domingue

Saint-Domingue was the French-held part of the island of Hispaniola, also called Santo Domingo, in the West Indies. (This island today comprises Haiti and the Dominican Republic.) Because French colonial policy toward children of mixed race was somewhat more liberal than that of the other European colonial powers, there were many free, literate blacks (called *gens de couleur*, or "people of color") on Saint-Domingue, who sought equality with the ruling whites. Some of those *gens de couleur* had actually fought with the Patriots in the American Revolution as volunteers alongside French troops at the siege of Savannah, Georgia.[11]

Shortly after the American Revolution, France also had a popular revolution, which encouraged aspirations of liberty and equality in its colonies. As the slaves' struggle for equality with the white planters grew more desperate, the *gens de couleur* on Saint-Domingue decided to help their cause by arming the slave population. The result was a slave rebellion that at first failed, followed by a complicated, fifteen-year-long war. Many refugees and exiles from Saint-Domingue fled to the United States. In 1795, Toussaint L'Ouverture took over the leadership of the slave revolution in Saint-Domingue. Finally—at the cost of over sixty thousand lives—the first black republic of Haiti was established in 1804 under the leadership Jean-Jacques Dessalines.

Word of the struggle reached American slaves by way of refugees, black seamen, and slaves from Saint-Domingue sold to slaveholders in the South. One result was a series of near-rebellions in the South throughout the 1790s. Historian Sylvia Frey mentions incidents in Virginia, North Carolina, Georgia, and South Carolina in the years 1792 to 1798.[12]

This portrait of Toussaint L'Ouverture appeared on a 1938 poster for the play *Haiti.*

A literate slave named Gabriel "Prosser" (from the Prosser farm) led a rebellion in 1800 in and around Henrico County and Richmond, Virginia. When the scheduled revolt was delayed by a torrential rainstorm, two anxious slaves betrayed the rebels, and the plot was crushed. Gabriel nearly escaped by boat, but was captured and hanged. In 1811, three to five hundred slaves started to march on New Orleans from around St. John the Baptist Parish in Louisiana. Relatively few details are known about this revolt. It was probably led by Charles "Deslondes" (from the Deslondes plantation), a refugee from Saint-Domingue.

Slaveholders in the South were frightened by the success of the Haitian revolution, by other unsuccessful revolts in the Caribbean, and by the many small rebellions throughout the southern United States. They feared that slaves were becoming less and less tolerant of their bondage. They were absolutely right.

THE ANTISLAVERY MOVEMENT GATHERS FORCE

I N THE SOUTH, THE FEAR OF BLACK REBELLION caused many states to pass laws restricting both slaves and free African Americans. New regulations made it more difficult for free African-American artisans (skilled workers) and seamen to be hired and to travel freely.

The slave revolts in other countries and the early revolts both north and south occurred before there was an anti-slavery movement that was labeled as "abolitionist." (The word *abolition* means the act of abolishing, or doing away with.) However, literate African Americans who entered the ministry helped start the antislavery movement. From the middle 1700s, free African-American antislavery activists used printed materials to get their message across. Pamphlets were cheap to produce, easily transportable, and could be displayed and distributed publicly.

Daniel Coker was a black minister from Virginia. He

published one of the very few public antislavery protests that originated in the South. His pamphlet "A Dialogue Between a Virginian and an African Minister" presents a calm and reasoned imaginary conversation between a slave owner and an antislavery cleric. Each of them claims to be entitled to the slave's liberty. "Now, the question is, who has the best claim?" his minister asks.[1]

James Forten, a wealthy free African-American sail-maker, published a "Series of Letters by a Man of Colour" in 1813. Between its publication and his death in 1842, he was a strong supporter of antislavery, and later abolitionist, activities and publications.

The Rise of Black Churches

In 1780, Lemuel Haynes became the first black minister licensed to preach by a predominantly white denomination. A few years later, in 1785, he was ordained by the Congregational Church of West Hartford, Connecticut. He became the first black minister to pastor a primarily white congregation, first in Torrington, Connecticut, and later in Rutland, Vermont. He received the first honorary degree ever given to an African American, from Middlebury College in 1804.

Churches were at the heart of the rising feelings of African-American independence in the North. The two principal black churches were founded in New York and in Philadelphia in the years following the Revolution, and both were formed out of the dissatisfaction of black church members with their role in predominantly white churches.

In Philadelphia, the founders of the African Methodist Episcopal Church, Richard Allen and Absalom Jones, were both former slaves who had managed to purchase their freedom. Upset at their second-class treatment as members at St. George's Methodist Church, they raised money for their own church. The African Episcopal Church of St. Thomas opened on July 17, 1794. While Jones was happy to be part of the Episcopal Church, Allen was a committed Methodist. He soon opened the rival "Mother Bethel" African Methodist Episcopal Church, serving a more working-class population than the "elite" St. Thomas. Allen preached in several cities and was a strong defender of racial equality. In 1816, Allen's church united with churches

in several other cities to separate from the white Methodist denomination, and formed the independent African Methodist Episcopal Church, with Allen as its first bishop.

In New York, a sexton named Peter Williams led a group of dissatisfied

Before he cofounded the African Methodist Episcopal Church, Richard Allen helped start the Free Black Society, which provided services, in 1787.

black church members out of the John Street Methodist
Church in 1796. They received permission to meet for wor-
ship, and five years later were independently chartered as
the "African Methodist Episcopal Church of New York City
called Zion." Their founders included James Varick, for
whom a major street in downtown New York was named.
The AME Zion Church voted to separate themselves from
white Methodists in 1820.

The American Colonization Society

The American Colonization Society held its first official
meeting on New Year's Day of 1817. The Reverend Robert
Finley's 1816 pamphlet, "Thoughts on Colonization," had
gained support from such major figures as Supreme Court
Justice Bushrod Washington, Speaker of the House Henry
Clay, lawyer (and composer of "The Star Spangled Banner")
Francis Scott Key, and Senator Daniel Webster. Its purpose
was to encourage free African Americans, against whom,
Clay said, there would always be "unconquerable preju-
dices," to leave the United States and live in Africa. Even
before the Society was founded, Paul Cuffe, a free African-
American sea captain, had in 1815 transported thirty-eight
African Americans to Sierra Leone, Africa, at his own
expense. Cuffe, a prominent black Quaker, had earlier led a
fight by free African Americans in Massachusetts for the right
to vote. He then began to promote the idea of colonization.
He might have become a major force in the abolition movement, but he died in 1817. He was regarded as a hero at

rising African-American institutions, such as the New York African Institution.

"The response North and South [to colonization] was generally favorable. Free blacks, however, reacted unfavorably," says historian C. Edward Skeen.[2] While colonization appeared on the surface to be a solution to America's racial problems, it masked a fear in its white proponents of an expanding free African-American population. Initially, some antislavery advocates, both black and white, embraced the idea of colonization. The United States Congress even donated $100,000 in 1822 toward the founding of Liberia, on the west coast of Africa, as a destination for the "colonizers." However, comments Skeen, "by the 1830s abolitionists questioned whether the colonization society was a benevolent association at all, because of its indifference to race prejudice and slavery."[3]

Against Colonization

Most free African Americans were not interested in colonization. Colonizers tried to convince them that they would never be treated democratically in the United States. By 1830, however, only about fifteen hundred free African Americans had made the trip back to Africa.[4] By then, most free African Americans had been born in the United States. Africa was a distant land where they had never lived, and where strange languages were spoken. Why would they want to leave their own country for a place they did not know?

Peter Williams, an African-American pastor of the

St. Philips Episcopal Church in New York, fought against colonization in his well-reasoned sermons. "Though delivered from the fetters of slavery, we are oppressed by an unreasonable, unrighteous, and cruel prejudice, which aims at nothing less than the forcing away of all the free coloured people of the United States for the distant shores of Africa," he preached on July 4, 1830. ". . . We are NATIVES of this country, we ask only to be treated as well as FOREIGNERS. Not a few of our fathers suffered and bled to purchase its independence; we ask only to be treated as well as those who fought against it."[5]

The first black newspaper, *Freedom's Journal*, was formed in 1827 by publishers and editors John Russwurm and Samuel E. Cornish. Russwurm had been the first African-American graduate of Bowdoin College in Maine. These two men urged all African Americans to contribute articles about their experiences of discrimination, their schools and social organizations, their views on colonization, and their opinions about slavery.

David Walker's *Appeal*

The first published writing that advocated open revolt against slavery was a pamphlet put out by David Walker, a free African-American clothing merchant in Boston. Walker, born free in the South, became a lecturer for the Massachusetts General Colored Association. Walker began to write for *Freedom's Journal*, but John Russwurm found Walker's opinions too extreme.

Walker confirmed this radicalism when he published *Walker's Appeal in Four Articles*, a pamphlet urging "coloured citizens" to use any means possible to attain equality. "Americans, I declare to you," he wrote, "while you keep us and our children in bondage, and treat us like brutes, to support you and your families, we cannot be your friends . . . . And wo, wo, will be to you if we have to obtain our freedom by fighting."[6]

Walker's pamphlet became so popular that it was reprinted three times. It was sold all over New England and the territories, and was distributed by African-American seamen down the coast to the southern states. "Crates of Walker's 'Appeal' circulated in Virginia, Georgia, and South Carolina in the early 1830s," write Newman, Rael, and Lapsansky.[7] It was so notorious that it was banned by law in Georgia, North Carolina, Mississippi, and Louisiana, where severe punishments were decreed for anyone who was found reading it. Pro-slavery advocates offered a reward of one thousand dollars for Walker's death. It may have worked: He died, mysteriously, a year later.

Many of the antislavery advocates in New England, both black and white, were horrified by Walker's appeal for violent action. They instead pressed their fight for alternative, more peaceful strategies. Nearly continual news of rebellions in the British and French Caribbean colonies made it clear that change was unavoidable. The antislavery, antiviolence opinion transformed during the 1830s into the "abolitionist" movement.

CHAPTER 5

ABOLITIONISTS ORGANIZE

WILLIAM LLOYD GARRISON, A LEADER OF THE abolitionist movement, published the first issue of his newspaper, *The Liberator*, in 1831. "The first day of [*The Liberator*'s] publication, January 1, 1831, is often taken as the point of departure for the new abolitionism," states historian William Lee Miller.[1]

Garrison had joined the ranks of antislavery voices through the urging of Quaker Benjamin Lundy, who traveled widely speaking about slavery. Though the young writer Garrison was already a reformer, Lundy convinced him that slavery was the institution most in need of reform. Garrison soon became impatient with Lundy's patient gradual approach to emancipation. Garrison wrote about the abolition of slavery in that first issue, "I will not equivocate—I will not excuse—I will not retreat a single inch—AND I WILL BE HEARD."

In the same year that Garrison started *The Liberator*, a

Before he started publishing *The Liberator*, William Lloyd Garrison had been jailed for his attacks against slave traders in Benjamin Lundy's newspaper. Lundy was an antislavery Quaker who got Garrison interested in the cause.

literate slave named Nat Turner led an "army" of seven slaves in a rebellion in Southampton County, Virginia. By the time Turner's army had grown to forty slaves, sixty whites had died. All the rebels were captured and hundreds of blacks, free and slave, were tortured and murdered in reprisals for the massacre.

Garrison had condemned Walker's appeal for its call to violence, and felt the same way about the actual violence of Nat Turner's rebellion. However, Garrison, because of his "immediatism," became the focus of heated opposition from frantic southerners frightened by the prospect of wider slave rebellion. As historian William Lee Miller says, "Garrison and his new publication came to be notorious—condemned and denounced particularly in the South—in part by confusion and association with these events by which its beginning was bracketed."[2]

The consequence of Walker's pamphlet and Turner's

rebellion was a further tightening of laws in the South preventing free movement of slaves, and especially of free African Americans. It became harder and harder for slaves to achieve manumission (the legal grant of freedom), often requiring an act of the state legislature. Southerners suspected, correctly, that "some free Negroes lent manumission papers to runaways to facilitate their escape. The runaway would then mail back the paper from the free states," says historian Eugene Genovese.[3] Of course, the free African-American person was taking a terrible chance. Losing manumission papers meant that he or she could be thrust back into slavery at any moment. Many free blacks heroically took that risk throughout the slave states.

Meanwhile, abolitionism was growing stronger in parts of the North. New England, cities in New York, such as Rochester, and towns in Ohio, such as Oberlin, became centers of abolitionism and stops on the Underground Railroad. The decade from 1830 to 1840 saw the conversion of gradualists to "immediasts," as well as a new cry for

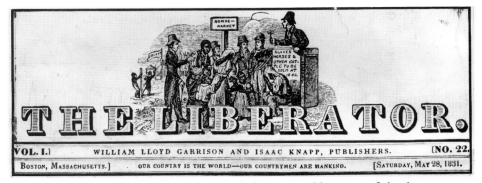

The Liberator **was one of the top abolitionist publications of the day.**

This depiction of Nat Turner's rebellion was made by a white artist. It was designed to emphasize the slaves' brutality in order to strengthen the case for slavery.

equality and integration that had been absent, particularly from the colonization movement.

"Since the beginning of the antislavery movement abolitionists had been confronted by arguments that Negroes belonged to a separate and inferior species of mankind," notes historian James M. McPherson. Abolitionists worked "tirelessly to combat those arguments,"[4] arguing that if slavery and racial discrimination were ended the former slave would become just as capable a member of society as any other citizen. The abolitionists knew that the belief in racial inferiority was one of the justifications for continuing slavery.

The now-famous poet John Greenleaf Whittier enlisted in the abolitionist cause in 1833. Whittier, a Quaker from Massachusetts, had always opposed slavery. His friend William Lloyd Garrison invited him to serve as a delegate to the convention in Philadelphia of what would become the American Anti-Slavery Society. Whittier, a gradualist who was just twenty-five years old in 1833, was reluctant to attend what would surely be a very controversial meeting. However, he not only attended the convention, he also became an avowed "immediast," and volunteered to draft an antislavery declaration to be presented to Congress. At age twenty-six, Whittier published an influential pamphlet, "Justice and Expediency," in which he condemned slavery and called for immediate emancipation.

The Philadelphia Convention was filled with sixty-three delegates, twenty-one of them Quakers. Their two prime objectives were "the entire abolition of slavery in the United States" and improving "the charter and condition of the people of color."[5] Among the delegates were several free black men who would become dedicated abolitionists, including Lewis Evans, James C. McCrummel, and James G. Barbadoes.

The Tappan Brothers and Theodore Weld

Two wealthy businessmen from New York, Arthur and Lewis Tappan, were very influential in abolitionist circles. The Tappan brothers' call for the formation of a national antislavery society was one of the events that led to the Philadelphia convention. Arthur Tappan, for whom southerners offered a $100,000 reward, dead or alive, humorously suggested that if the men who wanted him out of the way so badly would just deposit the money in his name in a bank, he might consider turning himself in.[6] Vandals broke into Lewis Tappan's house, hauled all the furniture outside, and smashed it to bits. These threats did not stop the determined benefactors. They enlisted another abolitionist friend, Theodore Weld, to find a site for a college to train clergymen for the new Western territories.

Theodore Dwight Weld, another Philadelphia convention delegate, was a Congregational minister who became the most prominent of the minister-abolitionists. Prior to 1831, Weld had traveled widely in the South, lecturing about education and temperance. He also talked informally to people about the moral problems of slavery. After David Walker's pamphlet and Nat Turner's revolt, however, the South became virtually closed to ideas and lecturers from the North. "The press, the pulpit, the colleges and seminaries, the bar [the legal profession] and the courts all collaborated to suppress dissent about slavery," according to historian Henry Mayer.[7] At the famous and respected Oneida Institute in western New York, Weld taught the sons of Lewis and Arthur Tappan. Weld became one of the leaders in the intense religious atmosphere at Oneida that condemned slavery as sin, and colonization as sin's ally.

Abolitionist Fever Mounts

As abolitionist fever mounted, those opposed to it set up roadblocks, such as refusing to house abolitionist meetings and terrorizing black schools. Abolitionist speakers were pelted with rotten eggs. Their meetings were interrupted by various groups of people including citizens who said they were offended. A hall in Philadelphia built especially to house abolitionist meetings was burned to the ground four days after it opened.

When George Thompson, a visiting English abolitionist, arrived to speak to the Boston Female Anti-Slavery Society in the fall of 1835, a group of people tried to kidnap him. When they could not find him, they instead kidnapped abolitionist William Lloyd Garrison, tied him up and marched through the streets. On the same day, a mob in Utica, New York, refused to let the convention of the Anti-Slavery Society of New York State hold its meeting. They broke up another meeting in a church to which the conventioneers had fled, and then destroyed the offices of an antislavery newspaper. A wealthy citizen living in nearby Petersboro, Gerrit Smith, hosted the convention. (Smith became a committed abolitionist on that night and was instrumental in helping scores of runaway slaves to freedom.) The events of that night also caused Wendell Phillips to call for abolition; he would become one of the great speakers for the abolitionist cause.

The first white abolitionist martyr (person killed for his or her beliefs) was Elijah Lovejoy, a minister and newspaper editor. Lovejoy had been forced to move three times when

A mob gathered outside the offices of the *Alton Observer*, Elijah Lovejoy's newspaper. They began to set fire to the building and shot and killed Lovejoy.

angry mobs had destroyed the printing presses for his anti-slavery newspaper. In Alton, Illinois, in the fall of 1837, he was shot and killed by a mob when he waved a pistol, trying to protect his fourth press. Some abolitionists—those who were morally or religiously opposed to violence—condemned Lovejoy's use of a gun. Many religious people called firearms "carnal weapons," and thought using them was sinful. Abolitionism was still founded on Protestant Christian religious beliefs, and abolitionists were undecided as to whether violence was acceptable.

Prudence Crandall, a schoolteacher and daughter of antislavery advocates, started a special school for

African-American girls in Canterbury, Connecticut, in 1831, and was supported by Garrison in *The Liberator.* Though lip service was given to the education of African Americans, having an actual African-American school in their town was too much for the citizens of Canterbury. The students were shunned in the town and then the school was cut off from deliveries of groceries, its water supply was spoiled, and a fire was set in the building.

The Grimke Sisters

Two of the most influential women in the abolitionist movement were Sarah and Angelina Grimke, daughters of a slaveholder in Charleston, South Carolina. By 1829, both sisters were living in Boston. When Angelina read about Garrison's being marched through the streets in 1835, she wrote him a letter saying that she would commit her life to ending slavery.

Garrison published her letter in *The Liberator.* Soon Theodore Weld, who encouraged women to speak at meetings that mostly included men, began to coach the Grimke sisters in public speaking. Though Angelina became the better abolitionist lecturer, both sisters wrote pamphlets condemning slavery, and used their southern connections to have the pamphlets smuggled into South Carolina. These were particularly aimed at raising the consciousnesses of southern women. The Charleston police ordered Angelina's immediate arrest if she should arrive in the city. The Grimke sisters also frequently lectured and traveled with leaders in the fight for women's suffrage (the right to vote), such as Lucretia Mott, Lydia Maria Child, Elizabeth Cady Stanton, and Susan B. Anthony.

The Grimke sisters took the unusual step of searching for their own black relatives. Henry Grimke, the sisters' brother, had fathered children with a slave named Nancy Webster. In his will, Henry had freed mother and sons; the sons, Archibald and Francis Grimke, had become pastors in Pennsylvania. Angelina and Sarah not only openly accepted their nephews, but also paid for their further education at Princeton Theological Seminary and at Harvard Law School. Francis went on to become a pastor of the Fifteenth Street Presbyterian Church in Washington, D.C., and Archibald was appointed U.S. Consul to Santo Domingo. He also became the first vice president of the NAACP when it was founded in 1909.

Sojourner Truth

In the mid-nineteenth century, Sojourner Truth emerged onto the abolitionist scene. Truth, who was born Isabella Van Wagenen, slave of a Dutch family in Ulster Country, New York, was sold several times and bore five children before she was freed in 1827 by the New York Gradual Abolition Act. She moved to New York City, worked as a housekeeper, and began preaching about religious issues on street corners.

She was a magnetic and passionate speaker, who made many friends and gathered many followers. She began, in

SOURCE DOCUMENT

Arriving at New Paltz, she went directly to her former mistress, Dumont, complaining bitterly of the removal of her son. Her mistress heard her through, and then replied–"Ugh! a fine fuss to make about a little nigger! Why, haven't you as many of 'em left as you can see to, and take care of? A pity 'tis, the niggers are not all in Guinea!! Making such a halloo-balloo about the neighborhood; and all for a paltry nigger!!!" Isabella . . . answered, in tones of deep determination–"I'll have my child again." "Have your child again!" repeated her mistress–her tones big with contempt, and scorning the absurd idea of her getting him. "How can you get him? And what have you to support him with, if you could? Have you any money?" "No," answered Bell, "I have no money, but God has enough, or what's better! And I'll have my child again." These words were pronounced in the most slow, solemn, and determined measure and manner. And in speaking of it, she says, "Oh my God! I know'd I'd have him again. I was sure God would help me to get him. Why, I felt so tall within–I felt as if the power of a nation was with me!"[8]

In her narrative (as dictated to Olive Gilbert), Sojourner Truth describes her efforts to get her son back. He had been sold away from her. The mistress Dumont uses the word "nigger," a very insulting word. However, Truth remained calm and eventually regained her son through the court system.

her orations, to combine abolitionism with women's rights, and strongly influenced the abolitionist movement to support women's rights, as well. Although she was illiterate and so could not write down her speeches herself, her admirers— including William Lloyd Garrison—wrote down many of her speeches and preserved them for history.

As the decade between 1830 and 1840 progressed, other abolitionists, black and white, gained prominence in the antislavery movement and continued the fight. Abolitionists were hated by many members of Congress. They flooded their representatives with petitions against slavery. All those signatures on all those petitions had a slow but growing effect. As early as 1836, former president John Quincy Adams refuted a resolution before Congress that stated, "Congress possesses no constitutional authority to interfere with the institution of slavery in any of the States of this Confederacy." According to historian Miller, Adams answered back that the resolution was "false and utterly untrue."[9] Adams, already an elderly man, was about to become a hero of the abolitionist movement because of another legal test of slavery. That test began off the shores of Long Island, New York, in 1839.

THE *AMISTAD* AND THE NEW DECADE

O N AUGUST 26, 1839, A RAGGED SHIP ANCHORED off the tip of Long Island. It was soon identified as the *Amistad*, a slave ship that had begun its voyage in Africa. Led by an African man called Cinque (sometimes also called Singbe or Joseph Cinquez), the captured Africans had revolted while sailing between two Cuban ports, killing the captain and the cook. Cinque had ordered the remaining crew to sail the ship back eastward to Africa. However, the mutineers were not knowledgeable sailors, so the crew had managed to trick them by turning the ship westward again every night. Although the crew could not get the ship back to Cuba, they hoped to make port somewhere in the American South. There, the Africans would have been recaptured, treated as slaves, and sold. The crew would have been paid for their cargo. Unfortunately for the crew, they missed the southern states

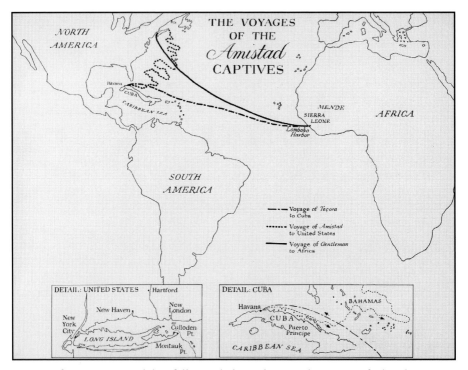

After Cinque and his fellow rebels took over the *Amistad*, the ship zigzagged nothward through the Atlantic. This was due to the Spanish crew sailing away from Africa during the night and toward Africa during the day.

and landed in New York, a free state, and home to many committed abolitionists.

The slaves could not tell their own story. Almost all the captives were from the Mendi-speaking lands of Africa, but no local officials spoke Mendi. Their revolt and detention in America caused an international dispute. The government of Cuba tried to portray the captives as slaves who had been in that country for a long time. Although slavery was still legal in the slaveholding states of America and in Cuba, the international slave trade between nations had been abolished by treaty in 1817. America had banned international slave trade in 1808. No country was permitted to kidnap Africans to be forcibly sold into slavery. If the captives had already been living as slaves in Cuba, the international ban on slave trading would not apply to them, and they would have to be returned to Cuba. Spain, which had sponsored the voyage, wanted them treated as criminals, mutineers, and murderers. Northern abolitionists thought that they had been kidnapped from Africa, and should therefore be freed.

The captives were jailed in New London, Connecticut, and charged with piracy and murder. Only after several months was a Mendi interpreter found, allowing the Africans to finally tell their tale: They were not long-time slaves. That meant they were free people who had been abducted when they arrived in the United States. How, then, could they be delivered into slavery?

The *Amistad* group became a major abolitionist cause. Lewis Tappan and Joshua Leavitt, editor of the influential abolitionist newspaper *The Emancipator*, became leaders in finding legal means to set the Africans free. Because the group was held captive in Connecticut, abolitionist faculty and students from the schools of law and divinity at Yale also became involved in the cause. Thousands of people paid twelve and a half cents each to file through the county jail in New Haven to look at the prisoners. Newspapers all over the North wrote about the plight of the *Amistad* captives.

President Martin Van Buren, who was running for re-election in 1840, had to be very careful about the case. To offend Spain and Cuba would cause diplomatic problems, and to offend the slaveholding South would risk his reelection campaign. But calling the Africans slaves would arouse even more abolitionist protest. Van Buren worked hard behind the scenes to accommodate Spanish and pro-slavery interests.

The Supreme Court Decides

As the case went to the Supreme Court, Tappan and Leavitt turned to John Quincy Adams, a former president of the United States, whom they knew supported an end to slavery. Adams did not know that he would be expected to actually try the case before the United States Supreme Court. He

"knew that many Americans were waiting for him to stumble and perhaps to fall. . . . in leading what amounted to an attack on the Van Buren

Before he was captured in West Africa, Cinque was being groomed to take over leadership of the Mendi village of Mani from his father.

administration."[1] He was seventy-four years old; he had not tried a case for over thirty years. Despite that, he spoke for four and a half hours on his first day before the court. When the Court reconvened a few days later, he spoke for another three hours. Adams pointed out that the *Amistad* captives were free people by the laws Spain itself had agreed to. There was no more transatlantic slave trade, so how could these people not be considered free to use force to resist kidnapping?

Supreme Court Justice Joseph Story announced the verdict on March 9, 1841. Adams wrote to Lewis Tappan, "The captives are free!"[2] John Quincy Adams had proved that the Constitution was, indeed, an appropriate place to deal with matters of slavery. He never sent a bill for his services to Lewis Tappan; John Quincy Adams had joined the ranks of the abolitionists. Although the decision was legally very narrow, both black and white abolitionists celebrated it as a major step toward emancipation.

It was almost a year before the thirty-five survivors of this long ordeal could return to Africa. After the Supreme Court decision, Cinque and others from the *Amistad* toured on the abolitionist lecture circuit to raise money for their passage home. At last, in November 1842, the *Amistad* mutineers sailed for their home in Sierra Leone, Africa.

Frederick Douglass

The year before the *Amistad* arrived in the United States, Frederick Douglass escaped from slavery to the North.

Douglass's fame as an abolitionist would equal that of William Lloyd Garrison. We know about his early days as a slave because of his brilliant way with both the written and spoken word, in speeches and in his three autobiographies.

Frederick Douglass was born a slave on a Maryland plantation and was raised by his grandmother, because his mother was sold away from the plantation before he was two years old. He spent the first eight years of his life on a plantation with a cruel master, and witnessed the torture and death of many in his slave quarters. However, he was sold away to the city of Baltimore. At first, his mistress there, Sophia Auld, was kind to him. She taught him the alphabet and how to spell short words. Unfortunately, when her husband found out about this, he became very angry. He not only forbade his wife to continue her teaching, but as recorded by Douglass in his first autobiography, *Narrative of the Life*, also told her, "A nigger should know nothing but to obey his master—to do as he is told to do. Learning would spoil the best nigger in the world. Now, if you teach that nigger how to read, there would be no keeping him. It would forever unfit him to be a slave."[3]

Douglass says that it was those harsh words that inspired him to continue reading by whatever means possible. His once-kind mistress became distant and stern, and the whole family worried that young Frederick might be sitting somewhere with a newspaper or book. "I now understood what had been to me a most perplexing difficulty—to wit, the white man's power to enslave the black man," wrote Douglass. "From that moment, I understood the pathway from slavery to freedom."[4]

Douglass made friends with poor white children of the neighborhood as he carried out his errands for the Auld family. Sometimes he brought with him bread, as these children often did not have as much to eat as he did in the Auld household. He always carried a book with him, and in exchange for friendliness and bread, he would get a lesson from it. Douglass taught himself to write by copying the names of parts of ships in a shipyard, and by challenging any boy whom he knew could write to a writing contest. During the contest, he could study how the unsuspecting teacher formed his letters. He also happened to get a book of speeches called *The Columbian Orator*. In it was a fictional dialogue between a master and slave, in which the slave convinces the master to free him. Douglass, now able to read and write, still wanted desperately to be free.

A Cruel New Owner

Douglass was "inherited" by a member of the Auld family who proved to be a cruel master. Thomas Auld, according to Douglass, had no personal honor, and never did one thing that would make anyone respect him. Being literate, Douglass had the respect of other slaves, but was feared by owners. Auld therefore "loaned" him to an even crueler

In addition to lecturing and publishing against slavery, Frederick Douglass was one of the many stationmasters on the Underground Railroad and often spoke with Abraham Lincoln about slavery.

slave owner, a Mr. Covey, who was known for breaking young slaves.

Years later, in an expanded autobiography, *Life and Times of Frederick Douglass, Written By Himself*, Douglass includes a chapter called "The Last Flogging." He describes how Covey beat him, and deprived him of sleep and food until "I was completely wrecked, changed and bewildered, goaded almost to madness at one time, and at another reconciling myself to my wretched condition."[5]

One day, after having been severely beaten, Douglass suffered what was probably heatstroke while feeding wheat to a threshing machine. Although he was simply too weak to get up, Covey beat him for his supposed laziness. Covey finally tired, and Douglass managed to crawl off into the woods, where he fell asleep. When he awoke, he went to his master, Thomas Auld, to ask that he be brought back, as Covey had gone too far. Auld refused, and sent him back. To

Mr. Gore once undertook to whip one of Colonel Lloyd's slaves, by the name of Demby. He had given Demby but few stripes, when, to get rid of the scourging, he ran and plunged himself into a creek . . . Mr. Gore told him that he would give him three calls, and that, if he did not come out at the third call, he would shoot him. The first call was given. Demby . . . stood his ground. The second and third calls were given with the same result. Mr. Gore then . . . raised his musket to his face, taking deadly aim at his standing victim, and in an instant poor Demby was no more.[6]

Frederick Douglass described the fate of the slave Demby. Mr. Gore successfully defended his actions to the master, Colonel Lloyd, and was not removed from his position as overseer.

escape seemed impossible—the land on which the farms were located was completely surrounded by water.

When Frederick Douglass finally returned, Covey pretended to ignore him. Then, coming up behind Douglass, he tried to tie his feet. "Whence came the daring spirit necessary to grapple with a man who, eight-and-forty hours before, could, with his slightest word, have made me tremble like a leaf in a storm, I do not know; at any rate, *I was resolved to fight!*" says Douglass.[7]

According to Douglass's story, for two hours he managed to keep Covey from striking him. Finally, the exhausted Covey said, "Now you scoundrel, go to your work; I would not have whipped you half so hard if you had not resisted."

"The fact was, he had not whipped me at all," writes Douglass. "I was a changed man after that fight. I was *nothing* before; I *was a man* now."[8] Douglass considers this the turning point in his life as a slave, because it made him once again believe in the possibility of liberty.

Douglass made one unsuccessful attempt to escape to the North, when he was eighteen years old. Two years later, in September 1838, he succeeded. With his new wife, Anna, he planned the escape in just three weeks. He impersonated a sailor, carrying an identity card either sold or loaned to him by a free black seaman.[9]

We know in detail about Douglass's years in slavery because he was a prolific writer and orator. But Douglass was just one of many slave heroes who resisted the rules of slavery, resisted the beatings, and took the final step of escape to freedom.

CHAPTER 7

THE REBELS AND
THE RUNAWAYS

SLAVERY CHANGED DRAMATICALLY IN THE United States after the invention of the cotton gin in 1793. The cotton gin was a mechanical device that combed the seeds out of the fibers of the cotton plant, making it much easier to spin those fibers into threads, and then cloth. This invention led to the large-scale cultivation of cotton as a "cash crop" in the Deep South—Alabama, Mississippi, Louisiana, and Arkansas.

The shift of agriculture from the eastern seaboard to the Deep South involved a huge movement of slaves to serve as the labor force for the new plantations. Historian Ira Berlin estimates that nearly a million slaves were forcibly moved from their homes, families, and communities between 1800 and 1860, in what he refers to as a "second middle passage."[1] To compare, the best estimates are that only half a million slaves were brought to the colonies from Africa over the two hundred years of the slave trade.

Within southern society, a myth arose that enabled slaveholders to justify their "peculiar institution." This ideology held that, because of their natural inferiority, "the proper—and most humane—place for black people was under the watchful supervision of a white master," says Berlin.[2] That this ideology was utterly false and mistaken only became apparent slowly, even to many white abolitionists.

Part of the reason that there was never a large-scale, successful revolt in the United States was that (unlike in the Caribbean) the slave population in the United States formed families and raised children. This resulted in the creation of community ties that, despite the cruelties of slavery, enabled the development of a slave culture different from, and stronger than, the African roots of the slaves. "The South had a balance of forces that was profoundly inhospitable to massive collective resistance," writes historian Peter Kolchin. "The absence of massive rebellion, however, hardly indicated passive acceptance of slavery."[3]

How Slaves Resisted

Slaves found ways to quietly assert their wishes, and to frustrate and exasperate their owners. Household goods were misplaced, tools left lying about, gates left open permitting livestock to escape, boats left unmoored to drift downstream. Slaves faked illness, and slowed down the pace of work. They also resorted to destroying the property of their masters, often through arson, and rarely they resorted to murder, by violence or with poison. Still more drastic measures included self-mutilation and even, in the most extreme cases, suicide. Slaves took from their masters, and felt justified in doing so. However, stealing from each other was a different matter, and was considered a crime in the slave quarters. All the methods of rebelling against enslavement, which carried with them the possibility of beatings and even more severe punishment, were really small acts of heroism.

In 1855, a slaveholder in Alabama reported that his slave, Tom, had stolen his master's turkey. When he was caught, he confessed without remorse. "When I tuk the turkey and eat it," Tom insisted, "it got to be part of me." Historian Eugene Genovese comments that if slaves "belonged to their masters—if they were in fact his chattels—how could they steal from him? They had only transformed his property from one form into another, much as they did when they fed the master's corn to the master's chickens."[4]

Frederick Douglass, again in his autobiography *The Life and Times of Frederick Douglass*, makes a very similar point. He says theft arose directly out of:

> the pitiless pinchings of hunger. So wretchedly starved were we that we were compelled to live at the expense of our neighbors, or to steal from the home larder . . . Considering that my labor and person were the property of Master Thomas, and that I was deprived of the necessaries of life—necessaries obtained by my own labor—it

was easy to deduce the right to supply myself with what was my own.[5]

Literacy among slaves was not encouraged, and few slaves managed to learn to read and write. Slaveholders were fearful of African-American literacy, and to some extent their fear was justified. Each of the three major slave uprisings was led by a literate African-American man: Gabriel "Prosser" in 1800, Denmark Vesey in 1822, and Nat Turner in 1831.

Though literacy was not permitted, music was. Slaves developed complex and sophisticated music, and used it to express a wide range of feelings—joy, despair, hope, exultation. Frederick Douglass claimed, "I have often been utterly astonished, since I came to the North, to find persons who could speak of the singing, among slaves, as evidence of their contentment and happiness. It is impossible to conceive of a greater mistake." Though not all historians agree, Douglass claimed that "slaves sing most when they are most unhappy."[6]

House servants, who were often the slaves most trusted by their owners, could be adept at pretending to be simple and uninterested. They sometimes functioned as a spy network for the slave cabins. By pretending to be stupid, shy, or loyal in order to gain favors, many black slaves encouraged southern slaveholders to believe a false stereotype of slave capabilities. The slaveholders chose to think that when slaves lied and stole and worked slowly, it was evidence that their slaves were from an inferior race. The reality was that their slaves were often engaged in acts of resistance and rebellion.

It took great shrewdness and planning to passively resist without risking punishment. As historian Peter Wood points out, "slowness, carelessness, and literal-mindedness were artfully cultivated, helping to disguise countless acts of willful subterfuge as inadvertent mistakes."[7] When a new overseer came to a plantation, the field slaves banded together to test the man. Every trick was used to work against discipline. Kenneth Stampp records a story of the Florida plantation of George Noble Jones, where the slaves successfully resisted letting a new, harsh overseer discipline

Slaves in fields often purposely made mistakes or slowed their work in order to resist their oppressive owners.

them. " 'I regret to say,' the overseer reported to Jones, 'that I never have had as hard work to git cotton picked and that don in good order befor. It seames that those people was determine to not pick cotton.'"[8]

Slaves' daily resistance to slavery was not without cause. Repeated floggings provoked running away. Slaves often ran off to keep themselves from physically resisting their attackers, which would have meant even more severe punishment or even death. Eugene D. Genovese says that "slaves who would not submit to whippings existed in every part of the south."[9] Peter Kolchin further comments, "Slave owners . . . rarely described these confrontations in detail, and their precise frequency is impossible to gauge." To him, there appears to be "a surprisingly widespread pattern of small-scale confrontations."[10]

The most frequent and continual form of resistance to enslavement was running away. Slaves ran away for many reasons. Sometimes they went to see a spouse or parent or child. Sometimes they disappeared to the woods until the overseer's temper cooled down. Sometimes they just wanted time off. Sometimes, they tried to get completely away, to escape to the North, or to establish a free life in a city, or to find a community to live in. (The town of Timbuctoo, New Jersey, east of Philadelphia, was founded in 1820 by runaway slaves.)

"Maroon" Communities

Some runaways formed "maroon" communities deep in the woods and swamps. Maroons were found in North Carolina, Virginia, Florida, Louisiana, and Georgia. The Great Dismal Swamp, an area on the border of Virginia and North Carolina, provided a harsh, dangerous, but somewhat secure hideout for runaways.

Describing his life in a maroon community to a Union Army officer during the Civil War, Octave Johnson, just twenty-one years old, said that his community grew from thirty to three hundred runaways, living in the swamps outside New Orleans.[11] Though the settlement was only four miles behind a plantation, even the planters' dogs could not penetrate the swamp. The fugitives hunted for meat and traded it for corn meal with plantation slaves.

Runaway slaves often had to hide out in the woods or swamps. Sometimes they even created whole communities there.

Maroon communities in the United States began to disappear in the mid-nineteenth century, as the country expanded and better roads made it easier to penetrate the deep woods where runaways hid. By then, however, most slaves—especially in the states that shared a border with a free state—knew that if a runaway could escape to the North, there were people willing to help.

The Escape of the Crafts

Some people managed to run away to freedom by means of clever planning and fierce courage. William and Ellen Craft escaped by the ruse of having Ellen, who was very light-skinned, disguise herself as a young white gentleman. William, who was dark-skinned, posed as Ellen's servant. They traveled in these roles for four days, first-class, all the way from Georgia to Philadelphia. They solved one serious problem—that neither Ellen nor William could read or write—with a clever trick: Ellen, the "master," kept her right hand bandaged and in a sling, as if she had been hurt, to avoid having to sign hotel registers. As the story of their escape became known in the North—stories about them were published in *The New York Herald* and *The Boston Globe*—they became favorites on the abolitionist lecture circuit.[12]

Henry Highland Garnet, who became an influential Presbyterian minister and fiery abolitionist, was born into slavery. His father managed to get the entire family passes to a funeral in 1825, and they escaped to New York City.

These drawings of William and Ellen Craft appeared in William Still's *The Underground Railroad,* published in 1872. William Craft later wrote *Running a Thousand Miles to Freedom,* which describes his and his wife's journey.

Garnet attended African Free School, established by the New York Manumission Society in 1787. Responding to a notice in *The Liberator,* Garnet and two other students applied to the Noyes Academy in New Hampshire, which was looking to enroll African-American students. Having no money, they walked from New York to Canaan, New Hampshire. Unfortunately, an anti-integrationist mob drove them out of Canaan.

Garnet went on to attend the Oneida Theological Institute, where Beriah Green, a teacher and abolitionist, encouraged him to fight for full and immediate emancipation. Though Garnet at first resisted the idea of violent action, he began to despair of any other way that would be effective.

Garnet's Call To Rebellion

In 1843, at the National Negro Convention in Buffalo, New York, Garnet delivered what became known as the "Call to Rebellion" speech, containing these words:

Brethren, arise, arise! Strike for your lives and liberties. Now is the day and the hour. Let every slave throughout the land do this, and the days of slavery are numbered. You cannot be more oppressed than you have been—you cannot suffer greater cruelties than you have already. *Rather die freemen than live to be slaves.* Remember that you are FOUR MILLIONS![13]

As a prominent minister, Garnet encouraged others to follow his lead. His cry became, "Let your motto be resistance! resistance! RESISTANCE!"[14]

Much later, during the Civil War, Garnet organized African-American troops for the North, and earned the honor of being the first African American to preach a sermon in the House of Representatives, in 1865. After the Civil War, he served as president of Avery College in Pennsylvania, and in 1881 was appointed U.S. ambassador to Liberia.

Another escaped slave whose life was filled with heroic achievements was Harriet Tubman. She was one of the most successful runaways to devote herself to helping others escape from slavery, and was instrumental in expanding the reach of the Underground Railroad.

ESCAPE FROM SLAVERY

A SIX-YEAR-OLD SLAVE GIRL NICKNAMED MINTY took a lump of sugar from a bowl on the dining room table, curious about the taste. Her mistress saw her and screamed at her. To avoid being whipped, Minty ran from the house and hid behind the pigpen. It was not the first time. Later, this little girl nearly died from pneumonia. Still later, while trying to protect another slave, she was struck in the head with a heavy iron tool by an overseer and was severely injured. She was in a coma for eight months, and throughout the rest of her life suffered "spells," during which she would just stop talking and for some moments look completely blank.

Minty, whose name was Harriet Tubman, ran away to the North in 1849. Tubman had heard the rumors about a network of antislavery supporters known as the Underground Railroad, who would hide escaped slaves as they made their way north. Tubman fled first to a Quaker

woman near her master's plantation in Maryland. The woman helped her to travel to freedom in Philadelphia.

Not content with only her own freedom, Tubman went back to the South nineteen times, sometimes disguised as a man. She was responsible for assisting in the escape of an untold number of slaves. Slaveholders set a bounty of forty thousand dollars on her (a huge fortune at that time). In 1852, threatened by the Fugitive Slave Laws, she moved her home and base of operations to St. Catharines, a town in Ontario, Canada, that welcomed fugitives from slavery.

Other Abolitionist "Escape Artists"

Harriet Tubman was not the only abolitionist who helped slaves flee to freedom at great personal risk. Calvin

Fairbanks, a former slave, helped by a white woman from Vermont known only as "Miss Webster," brought many slaves to freedom. "Miss Webster" would travel south and meet slaves who had been alerted by Fairbanks. These

Harriet Tubman would go on to work for the Union Army during the Civil War.

people posed as her servants and thus traveled north. Fairbanks spent seventeen years in prison for his "crimes." He boasted that the slaves he brought north were never caught.

Levin Coffin became known as "the president of the Underground Railroad," and helped more than three thousand slaves to freedom over the course of thirty-five years. He employed many freed slaves in his Underground Railroad operations, mostly as drivers in secret late-night rides. In 1876, he published his *Reminiscences*, one of the most substantial accounts of the activities of the Underground Railroad.

Henry "Box" Brown

William Still, a free black man born in New Jersey, helped with hundreds of escapes. In 1872, Still published one of the first authoritative accounts of the Underground Railroad. It included an account of the unusual escape of Henry "Box" Brown, from Richmond, Virginia, "an exploit that became a classic in Underground Railroad lore."[1]

Henry "Box" Brown had himself shipped from Richmond to Philadelphia in a specially built, cloth-lined box, two feet wide by two-feet, eight-inches deep by three feet long, relate historians Fishel and Quarles. He took some water and a few biscuits with him in the box, which had a small, concealed opening to let in air. His friends addressed the box and made sure that abolitionists in Philadelphia knew it was on its way. Although the box was

William Still helped chronicle the history of the Underground Railroad.

marked "This Side Up," the handlers on the overland express paid no attention, and for many miles he traveled upside down.

People working at the Anti-Slavery Society in Philadelphia managed to get the box delivered to their office without arousing suspicion. Everyone feared that when they opened the box, this daring slave would be found dead. However, when they knocked on the lid of the box, calling out "All right," his answer came back, "All right, sir!" According to Still's account, Brown rose up out of the box, dripping with sweat and "reached out his hand saying, 'How do you do, gentlemen?'"[2]

Slaves escaped constantly, although not usually as inventively as Henry "Box" Brown. John Fairfield, the son of a southern planter, arranged several mass escapes through Ohio. He once organized twenty-eight slaves into a make-believe funeral procession, and crossed the Ohio River to freedom not far from Cincinnati.

Josiah Henson, a slave who escaped from Maryland in 1825, went back several times to help others escape. He

first published his autobiography in 1849, and events from his life as a slave found their way into Harriet Beecher Stowe's book *Uncle Tom's Cabin*. She wrote to a correspondent that she "introduced some of [Henson's] most striking incidents into [the] story."[3]

Jane Lewis, a "conductor" at an Underground Railroad stop in New Lebanon, Ohio, rowed fugitives across the Ohio River. Many others, too numerous to list, and often anonymous, either escaped from slavery or helped others to escape. The southern slaveholders were getting a clear message, one they feared and hated: Slaves would escape whenever and wherever they thought they could safely do so.

Henry "Box" Brown emerged from the crate after the Philadelphia abolitionists opened it. He had endured a twenty-six hour trip from Richmond, Virginia.

After escaping from slavery, Josiah Henson and his family settled in Dawn, Canada.

Free African Americans in the North helped slaves escape in many ways. They served as stationmasters and conductors on the Underground Railroad. They raised money to help southern slaves buy their freedom. They pressured Congress, as well as state and local governments, to oppose slavery and support abolition. They ran schools and "vigilance committees" to guide, finance, and support newly arrived fugitives. Theodore Weld wrote to Lewis Tappan in 1834, "Of the almost 3000 blacks in Cincinnati more than three fourths of the adults are emancipated slaves, who worked out their own freedom. Besides these, multitudes [who are not in slavery] are toiling to purchase their friends . . ."[4]

More and more slaves were successfully sent on the Underground Railroad to the North or to Canada. Canada did not consider escaped slaves or those who helped them criminals. Canada had no treaty of extradition (return of escaped criminals) with the United States for fugitive slaves. Therefore, Canada was the only completely safe place for escaped slaves to go, and many Canadian towns were settled by runaway slaves. "According to one estimate, the South lost 100,000 slaves between 1810 and 1850" via the Underground Railroad.[5]

In the South, free African Americans could be sold back into slavery for the smallest misdeed—for violating a curfew, or simply for having inadequate papers. Or, he or she might just be kidnapped. No southern slave state wanted to have African Americans who were free. It was believed that they would set a bad example, or perhaps encourage the idea of freedom in their enslaved brothers and sisters. Some free African-American men in southern states actually bought their wives and children as slaves, to get around laws that forced newly freed slaves to leave the state immediately. If the free husband bought freedom for his wife and children, he would be forced to leave his home and livelihood, because his family, as newly freed slaves, would be obliged to leave the state.

The Fugitive Slave Laws Get Tougher

The first Fugitive Slave Act had been enacted in 1793. It had made it legal for slaveholders to recapture fugitive slaves in the free states and return them to slavery. However, it was difficult and expensive for slaveholders to track down the runaways. Although the law provided punishment for those who helped runaways, in practice this was hardly enforced in the free states. In fact, communities in many northern states enacted local laws that conflicted directly, and intentionally, with the federal law.

All that changed in 1850. Congress passed a new,

tougher Fugitive Slave Law, which made it easier for slave owners to recapture their "property." Slaves could be reclaimed on just the oath or affidavit of a slave owner or his or her representative, and federal officials were required to help them. No contradictory testimony was permitted at the hearing, and the suspected runaway could not testify. There was no appeal procedure. Stiff penalties were imposed on anyone who helped in an escape or who hindered a recapture. There was no time limit, so even runaways who had been settled in their new communities for years and years could be taken. The commissioners who heard the cases were paid ten dollars if they approved the capture, but only five dollars if they did not. Was there any reason for them not to favor re-enslavement?

"It was clear to all parties," writes historian Henry Mayer, "that the 1850 Fugitive Slave Law was not so much a remedy for the South's chronic runaway problem as it was a deliberate condemnation of the abolitionist agitation that had unsettled traditional politics."[6]

Abolitionists called the law the "Man Stealing Law" and the "Bloodhound Bill." They opposed it in whatever ways they could. Theodore Parker, an abolitionist who became prominent in the decade between 1840 and 1850, swore that he would do everything he could to rescue a fugitive.

When two slaveholders' agents came to Boston in 1849 looking for the famous runaways Ellen and William Craft, crowds followed the agents wherever they went and blocked their way. Parker hid the fugitives and tried to have

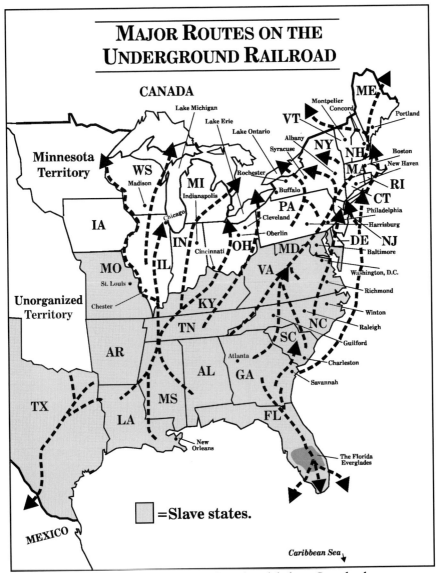

Most routes of the Underground Railroad led to Canada, however, some slaves did escape to Mexico or through the Florida Everglades swamp to a waiting ship on the coast.

the agents arrested. He was assisted by an African-American abolitionist named Lewis Hayden, a major "conductor" on the Underground Railroad, who had helped many slaves to freedom. The Crafts, fearful that their high visibility as abolitionist spokespersons would make them easy to capture, decided to leave the country.

In Boston, abolitionists put up this poster in 1851, a year after the law was enacted:

> CAUTION!! Colored people of Boston, one & all, you are hereby respectfully cautioned and advised, to avoid conversing with the Watchmen and Police Officers of Boston, for since the recent Order of the Mayor & Aldermen, they are empowered to act as Kidnappers and Slave Catchers . . . Therefore, if you value your Liberty. . . . Shun them in every possible manner.[7]

In the North, the new laws aroused tremendous opposition, even among people who did not think of themselves as abolitionists. With feelings running high over the issue of slavery in the new territories of California, Texas, New Mexico, and Arizona, northerners saw the law as a power grab by the South. They resented the intrusion by the federal government. They were angry that slaveholders' agents refused to notice the difference between free African Americans and runaway slaves.

Boston, because of its active abolitionist movement, was considered the safest place to avoid the increasingly tough fugitive slave laws. This, however, was about to change. In 1854, a fugitive slave named Anthony Burns was arrested and jailed in Boston. He had only been in Boston for two months when he was discovered by agents for his former master. Abolitionist sentiment being high in Boston, Burns was defended by Richard Henry Dana, a white abolitionist lawyer, and Robert Norris, a black abolitionist lawyer.

Wendell Phillips and Theodore Parker addressed the crowd at a protest rally on the steps of Fanueil Hall in Boston. With militia called in to keep Burns from being freed by the angry crowds, the judge ruled that the owner had the right to repossess Burns. "The revulsion of feeling throughout Massachusetts prompted the legislature to pass a more comprehensive personal liberty law . . . which practically made the [Federal] Fugitive Slave Law a dead letter in the Bay State," writes Benjamin Quarles.[8] The Burns case was a very public example of the many runaway slaves who were caught and returned to their masters in the slave states. Burns's arrest further divided the gradualists, who hoped that slavery would slowly fade away, from the militant abolitionists, who wanted immediate emancipation, at almost any cost.

Bleeding Kansas

In the same year Andrew Burns was hustled back into slavery, the Kansas-Nebraska Act of 1854 legalized the spread of slavery into territory where it had previously been

This poster depicts the various stages of Anthony Burns's story.

excluded. Since 1820, the Missouri Compromise had ensured the delicate balance of power between slave states and free states. The Compromise was that Congress accepted Maine into the Union as a free state, while at the same time it accepted Missouri as a slave state. It was understood that as the United States grew, slavery would be legal in any new states south of 36°30' latitude, while new states

SOURCE DOCUMENT

A MAN KIDNAPPED!

A PUBLIC MEETING AT
FANEUIL HALL!
WILL BE HELD THIS
FRIDAY EVEN'G,
May 26th, at 7 o'clock,
To secure justice for A MAN CLAIMED AS A SLAVE by a
VIRGINIA
KIDNAPPER!

And NOW IMPRISONED IN BOSTON COURT HOUSE, in defiance of the Laws of Massachusetts, Shall be plunged into the Hell of Virginia Slavery by a Massachusetts Judge of Probate!

BOSTON, May 26, 1854[9]

This sign was posted by supporters of Anthony Burns during the time of his trial.

north of that line would be free. New states would be admitted in pairs, one slave and one free, to maintain the balance of votes in the Senate.

The Kansas-Nebraska Act effectively ended that thirty-year balancing act. Bowing to the southern states' insistence that new states had the right to decide for themselves whether they would be slave or free, Congress permitted Kansas— which was north of the 36°30' line that everyone had accepted for thirty years—to vote on slavery. Because the Act also divided the Nebraska Territory into Kansas and Nebraska, it guaranteed that there would be at least one new slave state north of the former dividing line.

The Kansas-Nebraska act enraged people of every opinion in the North. Abolitionists saw it as an attempt to gain power by the slave states. Free African Americans absolutely opposed any further spread of slavery. New immigrants, who were arriving by the hundreds of thousands, especially from Ireland and Germany, were furious that they would have to compete with slave labor for their wages. The most unfortunate consequence of the Kansas-Nebraska Act was that both pro-slavery and antislavery advocates flooded into Kansas, to try to control the vote that was coming. Rival territorial governments were established. As the conflict grew violent, it led to a time of bloodshed, revenge, and chaos called "Bleeding Kansas."

Dred Scott Decision

The *Dred Scott* decision, a Supreme Court case handed down in 1857, also fed sectionalism and factionalism. Dred Scott was a slave who had sued for his freedom in the Missouri courts in 1847 after living for five years in the North, in Illinois and the free territory of Wisconsin. After almost ten years, his case came before the Supreme Court. The Court stated that Scott, as a slave, was "not intended to be included under the word 'citizens' in the Constitution." Justice Roger Taney also added that the Constitution gave Congress no right to regulate slavery at all, thus ruling that the Missouri Compromise of 1820 had been unconstitutional. "It would be difficult to exaggerate the destructiveness of the Dred Scott decision, for it emboldened the South as deeply as it embittered the North," writes Garrison biographer Henry Mayer.[10]

The decision favored the South, and even many of those in the North who were not devoted abolitionists or anti-slavery advocates were very upset. It created an abolitionist furor among the free African-American population, both in the North and the South. It also led directly to the most dramatic abolitionist challenge to slavery: the 1859 raid on Harpers Ferry.

9

JOHN BROWN'S
RAID

JOHN BROWN'S MOTHER HAD SUFFERED FROM
mental illness, and many of John Brown's actions
did not seem those of a totally stable individual. Why he
became such an ardent antislavery advocate is unclear.
However, he moved to Kansas in 1855 with five of his
grown sons specifically to fight against the proslavery
movement there.

Brown's attacks on the proslavery forces were violent,
and many abolitionists did not approve of his actions. At the
same time, because northerners were frustrated at pro-
slavery concessions to the South, some people admired a
man who literally took the law into his own hands.

Frederick Douglass had argued with William Lloyd
Garrison and other "immediasts" in the abolition movement over strategies for achieving emancipation. When
Douglas first met John Brown in 1848, he was impressed by
the simple way Brown lived. He also appreciated that

Brown treated him as a comrade in the cause of justice and liberation, not just as a poor ex-slave.[1]

Douglass was by this time a famous abolitionist orator. He had little patience with white people who wanted emancipation and black equality, but would not take a firm stand against slavery. Douglass listened to Brown talk about his plan for a slave rebellion that would establish a black state in the Appalachian Mountains of Maryland.

We do not know what Douglass thought of the practicality of Brown's plan. According to Douglass's biographer William S. McFeeley, he felt "there was no need to dampen the ardor of one white man who was ready to take action against slavery."[2]

Douglass's attitude toward Brown changed after Brown moved to Kansas. Brown and his sons murdered a proslavery father and his two sons. For Brown, the answer was often violence. Douglass had long been against violence.

Brown Plans His Attack

By 1859, Brown had evolved a new plan. He would capture the federal arsenal at Harpers Ferry, Virginia, and get weapons for his rebellion. Historian William S. McFeely wrote "Brown seemed to have forgotten his plans for establishing communities of fugitive slaves in the mountains. . . . Now Brown was obsessed with the idea of taking the Harpers Ferry arsenal . . . as the emblem of the military power of a government he had learned to hate. . . ."[3] Determined to enlist Douglass in his cause, Brown briefly moved into Douglass's house. When Douglass became aware of Brown's new revolutionary plans, he was dismayed. Douglass opposed the raid. He told Brown "that he was going into a perfect steel trap, and that once in he would not get out alive."[4]

John Brown enlisted twenty-two men for the raid, both white and black. They seized the arsenal at Harpers Ferry on October 16, 1859. Robert E. Lee, who later became the most famous Confederate Civil War general, commanded the detachment of marines that surrounded, then captured or killed all of the small army of insurrectionists.

John Brown was tried and sentenced to be hanged. He

John Brown's capture was depicted in *Frank Leslie's Illustrated.* Brown is the man on the ground to the right.

insisted in his last words to the court that he had never intended to kill or ruin property or raise an insurrection, but merely to free the slaves. "Now, if it is deemed necessary that I should forfeit my life for the furtherance of the ends of justice, and mingle my blood further with the blood of my children and with the blood of millions in this slave country whose rights are disregarded by wicked, cruel, and unjust enactments—I submit; so let it be done!"[5]

Divided Opinions

The night John Brown was hanged, free African Americans held solemn meetings all over the North. The next day— called by some African-American abolitionists "Martyr Day"—black-owned businesses in Boston, Philadelphia, and Detroit closed, and former slaves and free African Americans attended all-day church meetings in the free states.

White opinion, even in the North, was far more critical. Douglass, who was known to have admired Brown, was forced by the public outcry to flee to Canada. Enraged by Brown's violence, many public figures called for Douglass's imprisonment or execution for his association with Brown. From Canada, Douglass left for England on a previously scheduled lecture tour. Public opinion about Brown shifted wildly for the next several months. By the time Douglass returned a few months later, Brown had been executed. The charges against Douglass had been dropped. Abolitionists who had distanced themselves from John

In 1860, Frances Ellen Watkins married Fenton Harper, taking his name. After the Civil War, she wrote books and campaigned against alcohol and for the rights of women.

Brown's extremism had begun to transform him into a martyr to the cause of emancipation.

Ms. Frances Ellen Watkins—an African-American author, lecturer, and abolitionist who was acquainted with Brown's widow—wrote to her, "Not in vain has your dear husband periled all, if the martyrdom of one hero is worth more than the life of a million cowards." Watkins continued, "From the prison comes forth a shout of triumph over that power whose ethics are robbery of the feeble and oppression of the weak. . . ."[6]

Brown's raid polarized the country still further. "That great numbers of northerners mourned a reckless and murderous invader and condemned Virginia for punishing him infuriated the slaveholders' leadership even more than the raid itself," writes historian Henry Mayer.[7] Abraham Lincoln's words were prophetic: "I believe this government cannot endure, permanently half *slave* and half *free* . . . it will become *all* one thing or all the other."[8]

10

ON THE
ANTISLAVERY SIDE

THIRTY YEARS BEFORE THE BEGINNING OF THE Civil War, in 1831—the same year as the Nat Turner Rebellion—some European visitors recorded their impressions of the United States. The most famous of these commentators was Alexis de Tocqueville, a French citizen and court magistrate, who traveled with another young magistrate named Gustave Beaumont. Both men kept detailed journals, interviewed people, and wrote many letters home. They came to realize that although most Americans thought slavery was a necessary evil, they also thought that there was no way that a free black and a free white population could live together peacefully.

When Tocqueville interviewed John Quincy Adams, the former president, reports historian Louis P. Masur, he asked Adams if he believed slavery was "a great plague for the United States." Adams answered, "Yes, certainly. That is the root of almost all the troubles of the present and fear for the future."[1]

According to historian Louis P. Masur, Tocqueville and Beaumont observed, "Prejudice and segregation permeated the states, free as well as slave."[2] They noted that in Massachusetts, free blacks had the right of citizenship, but prejudice against them was so strong that their children could not attend white schools. In Philadelphia, white and black prisoners were separated even at mealtimes. In Baltimore, theaters, hospitals, churches, cemeteries and horse races were segregated. Though the Frenchmen had not intended to study the problem of race in America, they found it impossible to ignore.

Tocqueville wrote in a letter from Cincinnati:

> Slavery threatens the future of those who maintain it, and it ruins the State; but it has become part of the habits and prejudices of the colonist . . . and his immediate interest is at war with the interest of his own future and the even stronger interest of the country. . . . *Man is not made for slavery; that truth is perhaps even better proved by the master than by the slave.*[3]

The Beginning of the End of Slavery

Tocqueville and Beaumont, as well as many other observers of the United States in the thirty years before the Civil War, could see that slavery would eventually be abolished. It had already been abolished in many other countries around the world. Mexico abolished slavery in 1829. A steady stream of slave rebellions plagued the European colonies in the Caribbean: British Guiana, Barbados, Jamaica, Martinique, Antigua.[4] Slavery would be outlawed throughout the British Empire in 1834.

The years 1820 to 1850 were also a time of widespread civil unrest all over the world. The politics of independence and rebellion was in the air. "American slavery in 1835 was a formidable institution which appeared to be . . . invulnerable," says historian William Lee Miller, but it was not.[5]

From 1848 on, much of the conflict leading up to the Civil War—and the end of slavery—was waged in the political arena. The Republican party—Abraham Lincoln's party—emerged from the contradictory politics of the North in the 1850s. Thousands of immigrants arrived from Ireland, Germany, and Scandinavia, crowding the cities and settling the upper Midwest. White workers feared that immigrants or freed slaves would take their jobs away. States, both North and South, were concerned about the Federal government telling them what they could and could not do. Out of all these threads, the Republican party was born.

As the Republican party emerged, there was increasing talk in the South about seceding (withdrawing) from the federal government to protect the right of the southern states to make their own laws—including laws that preserved slavery. The conflicts between North and South over slavery, economic systems, immigration, and the rights of free African Americans seemed to make it impossible for the country to stay united.

The election of 1860 was hotly contested. The new Republican party nominated Abraham Lincoln in 1860. Abolitionists, both black and white, believed Lincoln to be better than the other candidates, but they did not completely support him. Lincoln believed that slavery should be ended gradually. Abolitionists had abandoned that idea long before.

H. Ford Douglas, an African-American abolitionist from Illinois and a former slave, expressed his reservations about Lincoln in speeches around the country. Douglas claimed that the Republican Party did not follow the abolitionist sentiments of Garrison, but "they want to take time . . . they want to do the work gradually." He quoted from a story by Washington Irving about a man who "wanted to jump over a ditch, and he went back three miles in order to get a good start, and when he got up to the ditch, he had to sit down on the wrong side to get his breath. So it is with these political parties; they are compelled, they say, when they get up to the ditch of slavery, to stop and take breath."[6]

The Southern States Secede

When Lincoln won the election in November 1860, things began to boil. Only three days later, South Carolina called a "secession convention." The next day, its two senators resigned from the U.S. Senate. On December 20, South Carolina seceded from the Union.

Intense negotiations failed to reach a compromise. In January, Mississippi seceded, then Florida, Alabama, Georgia, and Louisiana. In early February, the breakaway states formed a government. In early March, Lincoln took office. In early April, the Confederacy attacked a Federal garrison at Fort Sumter, South Carolina, and the Civil War began.

When the war actually came, what did prominent abolitionists, many of whom were against violence, think of it?

Theodore Weld, one of the major abolitionist speakers (and husband of Angelina Grimke) wrote, "I profoundly believe in the righteousness of such a war as this is, on its anti-slavery side."[7]

Sarah Grimke, once a strong opponent of violence, wrote in a letter to William Lloyd Garrison, "The war is the holiest ever waged, is emphatically God's war, and whether the nation will or not, He will carry it on to its grand consummation, until every American enjoys the rights claimed for them in our Declaration of Independence."[8]

The Anglo-African Weekly in New York wrote, "If you would restore the Union and maintain the government you so fondly cherish, make way for liberty universal and complete."[9]

Slaves Claim Their Freedom

Almost immediately after the war began—starting in May 1861—slaves began to free themselves by walking over to the Union lines. Soon, thousands of slaves headed for the front, wherever it happened to be. One witness, according to historians Fisher and Quarles, described these "mass migrations . . . as being 'like the oncoming of cities.'"[10] At first, the fugitive African-American men were used as workers—some two hundred thousand of them. African-American soldiers were not yet permitted in the Union army.

Abolitionists did not retreat once the southern states had seceded and the war was in progress. The new abolitionist cause became enlistment of black soldiers. Black civic organizations in the free states recruited militias and passed resolutions to enlist in the union cause. In Pittsburgh, free blacks formed the Hannibal Guards and volunteered to serve in the Western Pennsylvania Militia. The Guards' letter to the commander of that militia stated, ". . . although deprived of our political rights, we yet wish the government of the United States to be sustained against the tyranny of slavery, and are willing to assist in any honorable way or manner."[11] In Boston, Philadelphia, Cincinnati, and Cleveland, similar offers to join the war effort came from African-American groups. "White leaders recognized none of the black volunteer efforts and enlisted not a single African-American soldier," says military historian Michael Lee Lanning.[12]

Politicians were fearful that if black soldiers were enlisted in the Union Army, they would drive white soldiers away. They also feared that the slave-holding border states that had not yet seceded from the Union might be outraged

Slaves who fled to the Union lines often worked in Union Army camps during the Civil War.

and join the Confederacy in protest. Many people in the North were also convinced that the conflict would be brief, and not an all-out war. At first, enlistment was for only ninety days. Military personnel were told not to interfere with slavery as they brought troops to South Carolina.

Lincoln continued to insist that the war was not about ending slavery. He replied to Horace Greeley, powerful editor of the *New York Tribune*, "My paramount object in this struggle *is* to save the Union, and is *not* either to save or to destroy slavery. . . . I have here stated my purpose according to my view of *official* duty; and I intend no modification of my oft-expressed *personal* wish that all men every where could be free."[13]

Abolitionists continued to push for emancipation and enlistment of African-American men in armed services. Frederick Douglass was the principal spokesman for the absolute claim of African-American citizens to fight in a war that was about their rights—although Lincoln's administration was not yet willing to acknowledge that. Douglass predicted that whichever side first tapped this enormous resource of manpower would win the war. Jacob Dodson, an African-American maintenance worker in the Capitol building in Washington, offered himself and three hundred other African-American men to the cause. Lincoln declined.

The tide turned when it became apparent that the conflict, at first expected to be short and easy, was turning into a full-scale war. The Union Army was badly defeated by the Confederates in July 1861, at the Battle of Bull Run in Virginia. Other Confederate victories caused heavy casualties to the Union side. White northerners read about the horrible battles, and became more reluctant to enlist. Union army commanders, abolitionists, free African-American men, and fellow Republican Party members all pressured Lincoln to permit African-American recruits.

In addition, great pressure was put onto Lincoln to free the southern slaves, and not only by abolitionists. Freeing the slaves would earn Lincoln the approval of England and the rest of Europe. That would make it more difficult for the

Confederacy to gain recognition and help from those governments.

The Emancipation Proclamation

On June 22, 1862, President Lincoln told his cabinet that he planned to issue a proclamation that would free the slaves in those Confederate states still in rebellion on January 1, 1863. Lincoln's secretary of state, William H. Seward, advised him that it would be better to wait until the Union Army had won an important battle before he issued such a proclamation. Lincoln agreed, despite the protests from abolitionists and the increasing need for more manpower in the army.

The Battle of Antietam, on September 17, 1862—a successful battle for the Union side—offered Lincoln a chance to act. He warned the Confederacy that if they did not concede the war, the government of the United States would declare their slaves free. The Confederates ignored this ultimatum, and on January 1, 1863, Lincoln issued the Emancipation Proclamation. Strangely, the proclamation did not immediately free any slaves. That was because it applied only to the territories occupied by the Confederacy, which the Federal government did not yet control. The proclamation did not apply in the slaveholding territories that had not seceded—for example, Kentucky and Maryland—which were under Union control. As the war went on and the Union controlled more territory, more slaves were freed.

The day the Emancipation Proclamation was issued, free African Americans and abolitionists held public meetings all over the free states to celebrate the news. At the Tremont Temple in Boston, Frederick Douglass was one of the speakers to the crowd that had gathered to await the news that Lincoln had definitely signed the Proclamation. Douglas wrote of the event, "Eight, nine, ten o'clock came and went and still no word. A visible shadow seemed falling on the expecting throng, which the confident utterances of the speakers sought in vain to dispel."[14] When word finally came that, indeed, the Proclamation was real, the crowd broke into wild shouts and laughing and crying. Over at the fashionable Music Hall, where William Lloyd Garrison heard the news, the largely white audience cheered wildly, first for Lincoln and then for Garrison.[15]

Though Lincoln conceived of the Emancipation Proclamation as important for military success, it took on a life of its own. Despite its limitations, it was celebrated openly by black people in the North, and privately by slaves in the South. As Fischel and Quarles explain, it "changed the whole tone and character of the war, becoming a fresh expression of one of man's loftiest aspirations—the quest for freedom."[16] It also offered free African Americans the invitation so many had been waiting for—to enlist in the Union Army.

F R O M S L A V E T O S O L D I E R

BY THE END OF THE CIVIL WAR, 180,000 African-American soldiers had served the Union in nearly five hundred military engagements. Former slaves made up more than three quarters of the African Americans enlisted in the Union Army. Nearly seventy thousand former slaves and free African Americans died fighting for a country that had only reluctantly accepted their help.[1]

The Emancipation Proclamation encouraged the enlistment of freed African Americans all over the South. Black enlistment in the North quickly followed. John A. Andrew, abolitionist governor of Massachusetts, lobbied the War Department to organize African-American men of his state into military units. Permission was granted, but the two units authorized had trouble with recruitment—there were not that many black men in Massachusetts, and most of them had good work from the war economy.

Frederick Douglass, with his vivid style of speaking and

dramatic appeal, came to the rescue. Many other leading African-American abolitionists, among them William Wells Brown, J. W. Loguen, and J. Mercer Langston, also spoke out for enlistment. Volunteers began to come forward, and on May 28, 1863, the Fifty-fourth Massachusetts Infantry Regiment, under the command of Robert Gould Shaw, marched through huge crowds of cheering people in Boston. A few weeks later, the Fifty-fifth Regiment, under the command of Norwood P. Hallowell, followed the Fifty-fourth to battle. Over the next several months, African-American regiments from Rhode Island, Connecticut, Pennsylvania, Ohio, Illinois, Indiana, and Michigan also formed and joined.

The First Black Regiment Joins the War

The 54th Regiment engaged in battle at Fort Wagner, South Carolina, on July 18, 1863. Overwhelming numbers of Confederate soldiers defended the fort, and the majority of the regiment, including Shaw, was killed. The great bravery of one African-American soldier, Sergeant William H. Carney, age twenty-three, gained him the Medal of Honor. Each army unit had a regimental color-bearer, who carried their flag. Company C's color-bearer was killed early in the battle, and Carney took the flag and led the charge against the Confederate lines. Though wounded twice, he insisted on carrying the flag when his unit was driven back. The remaining men in his company cheered loudly when he returned to the lines, saying, "The flag never touched the ground, boys."[2]

William Carney became a Civil War hero.

The battle at Fort Wagner convinced most Union military strategists that recruiting African-American soldiers was a very good idea. General Ulysses S. Grant wrote that, along with emancipation, African-American soldiers in the military was "the heavyist [sic] blow yet given the Confederacy. . . . By arming the Negro we have added a powerful ally. They will make good soldiers and taking them from the enemy weakens him in the same proportion they strengthen us."[3] The successful example of the 54th Massachusetts led to other African-American units being given serious combat duties. *The New York Tribune* commented that if the African-American soldiers of the 54th had not proven their worth, the war might have gone on for at least a year longer.[4]

Despite the bravery and loyalty of African-American Union soldiers, they continued to face prejudice. This included lower pay than even the lowest-ranking white soldier. Once again, black and white abolitionists, who had

Many northern whites held the racist view that blacks were fearful. The storming of Fort Wagner proved to skeptical whites that blacks were brave in battle.

fought for the inclusion of black units in the war, now joined black soldiers' fight for equal pay. Yet even after pay was equalized, African-American troops were subjected to racism. Very few had the chance to become officers. No black officer ever led white soldiers.

Black Naval Heroes

It was not only through the army that African-American free men and emancipated slaves were involved in the Civil War. About twenty-nine thousand African-American seamen engaged in battles. The navy Medal of Honor was awarded to Joachin Pease, for his participation as a gunner, on June 19, 1864, in the sinking of the Confederate raider *Alabama* off the coast of France. The Medal of Honor was also awarded to African-American sailors Robert Blake, John Lawson, and Aaron Anderson for bravery under fire.

William Tillman, an African-American sailor aboard the Union schooner *S. J. Waring,* sailing from New York to South America, engaged in a dramatic rescue of his ship. The Confederate ship *Jeff Davis* captured *S. J. Waring,* and took all its crew aboard their ship except for Tillman and two others as cooks and stewards. Placing five Confederate sailors on the *Waring,* they set sail for Charleston, South Carolina. The ship was intended for the Confederate navy, and its African-American sailors were to be sold back into slavery.

In the middle of the night of July 16, 1861, Tillman and his companions killed three of the Confederate sailors with an ax, and captured the other two. He and his shipmates sailed the *Waring* and all its cargo back to New York, the American flag waving from its mast.

Captain Robert Smalls

Robert Smalls became the most famous African-American sailor to sail a ship to Union lines, and the only African-American sailor to attain the naval rank of captain. On May 13, 1862, Smalls and seven other slaves working on the three-hundred-ton Confederate steamer *Planter* were left on board as white sailors left the ship to go ashore. They brought their own families secretly on board, and Smalls

Robert Smalls (pictured with the *Planter*) was a congressman from 1875 to 1879 and from 1882 to 1887.

and his fellow-sailors sailed out of Charleston harbor right to the Union blockade. With a white bedsheet hoisted, they delivered their valuable cargo to the Union captain. Smalls joked, "I thought the *Planter* might be of some use to Uncle Abe."[5] Smalls and his crew received their freedom, and payment for the ship and its cargo. He became a valuable pilot for the Union navy, helping navigate along the South Carolina coast and around its rivers and canals. After the war, Smalls educated himself, and in 1876, served the first of five terms in the South Carolina Congress.

Black Women in the War

It was not only in battle that African-American heroism helped the Union war effort. Sojourner Truth and Harriet Tubman, both former slaves, worked as nurses in the North.

The Contraband Relief Society ("contraband" was the word applied to southern slaves who escaped to Union lines), consisting of forty African-American women who had been slaves, helped fugitive slaves in Washington, D.C. One of the Society's members, Charlotte Forten (granddaughter of early antislavery advocate James Forten), traveled to any region that flew the Union flag to teach reading and writing.

Susie Baker, an escaped slave who had been secretly educated by a free African-American woman, was first employed by the Union army as a laundress, until she was discovered to be both literate and an excellent nurse. When she married Edward King, an African-American soldier fighting for the Union, she went with him as a nurse and teacher for the soldiers in her husband's unit. Her book, *Reminiscences of My Life in Camp with the 33rd U.S. Colored Troops*, published in 1902, is the only known personal account of an African-American woman's war experiences.

As the war dragged on, the Confederacy considered emancipating their own male slaves so they could fight in the Confederate cause. Already, slaves who were taken to war by their masters formed the majority of the supporting labor force. Meanwhile, slaves who had been left behind on their plantations, often under the management of women who were not used to exercising such authority, became more and more independent. Much too late, President Jefferson Davis decided to enlist three hundred thousand slaves in the Confederate army, promising them emancipation (if the owners agreed).

After the War

Before any black troops could fight in the Confederate cause, however, the war ended. Lee surrendered to Grant at Appomattox Courthouse, Virginia, on April 9, 1865. In Georgia, Confederate general Joseph Johnston surrendered to Union general William Tecumseh Sherman on April 26, 1865. The very last Confederate troops surrendered on May 26, 1865.

African-American regiments were among the last to be dissolved, as they had entered the war late. Many African-American soldiers stayed in the army, but often were assigned to units that were sent out west, beyond the Mississippi River. These frontier assignments appeased those white people who worried about armed blacks in their communities. However, some African-American troops remained as occupation forces in the South for a short time after the war—in part as a strategy to remind southerners of what the war had accomplished.

With the ratification of the Thirteenth Amendment to the Constitution, on December 6, 1865, abolitionists and slave resisters had achieved their aim—slavery had been abolished. Eric Foner reports an exchange between William Lloyd Garrison and Frederick Douglass: "My vocation as an abolitionist, thank God, is ended," declared Garrison.

Douglass replied, "Slavery is not abolished until the black man has the ballot."[6]

The assassination of Abraham Lincoln, on April 14, 1865 just five days after Lee's surrender, had been a terrible blow to former slaves, who had begun to think of Lincoln as their greatest hope for voting rights as free American citizens. No one knows how Lincoln, a gradualist and a compromiser, might have guided the country after the war.

Emancipation, the end of war, and the end of secession did not end the debate over the treatment of African Americans. That debate centered on what should be done about freed slaves. Should they be treated as ordinary citizens capable of fending for themselves, or did they need special treatment and assistance from the government because of their former servitude? Both black and white people argued on each side of the issue. Ultimately, the government created the Bureau of Refugees, Freedmen, and Abandoned Lands, known as the Freedmen's Bureau, which was empowered to regulate "all subjects" related to the condition of freed slaves in the South.

African-American leaders—community leaders, religious leaders, political leaders—worked tirelessly to try to convert emancipation into permanent change. They formed separate African-American social organizations, such as churches and clubs, and pressed for inclusion in civic activities, such as juries and elections. African-American abolitionists such as George T. Downing, John Mercer Lanston, and Frederick Douglass created an African-American Congressional lobby to solidify gains in civil rights, especially the right to vote. Former abolitionists continued to fight for civil rights, including education, social and legal equality, and an end to discriminatory laws (even in northern states). After a long debate in Congress, the Civil Rights Act of 1875 was passed, though without some of its more important clauses, including integrated schools.

R. H. Cain was an African-American minister and politician from South Carolina and head of the Emmanuel African Methodist Episcopal Church of Charleston, one of the largest churches in the South. He addressed the speaker of the House of Representatives in 1872, during the first debates over the Civil Rights Act:

> Are there not five millions of men, women and children in this country . . . whose rights are as dear and sacred to them, humble though they be, as are the rights of the thirty-odd millions of white people in this land. . . . All we ask of this country is to put no barriers between us, to lay no stumbling blocks in our way, to give us freedom to accomplish our destiny. . . . Do this, sir, and we shall ask nothing more.[7]

This impassioned debate might be said to be still going on. Although the civil-rights movement of the 1950s and 1960s created many changes, today's civil rights advocates feel that still more changes are needed.

In a book called *What If 2*, which presents essays on major events in history and asks the question what if this or that did or did not happen, political commentator Tom

Wicker asks the question, "What If Lincoln Had Not Freed the Slaves?" What if our democracy

had failed, in its most fundamental test, to strike off those chains? Then the twelve per cent of Americans who are black would have to live with the knowledge that their forebears were not freed from bondage by crusade, by the willingness of a generation "touched by fire" to sacrifice its lives and futures, by the greatness of a leader martyred not least for his proclamation of brotherhood.

But Wicker goes on to say that, Lincoln did, after all, help free the slaves and in doing so "responded not just to the pressures of his era but—as if to a vision—the needs of later times, into the present and on into the future . . . it began the 'unfinished work' that Lincoln was to define at Gettysburg: a 'new birth of freedom' in a nation 'conceived in liberty' but not yet devoted to it."[8]

It takes courage and heroism to change situations that are obviously in need of change. Many slaves and abolitionists, both black and white, showed that heroism. They fought against and resisted slavery in a number of ways. They inadvertently brought about a war that, though terrible, put an end to slavery in the United States. African Americans flocked to the ranks of the Union Army to help win this war. While the United States still works toward full racial justice and full racial equality, the work of thousands and thousands of individuals has brought the country this far. Full equality is truly, as Lincoln said in his immortal Gettysburg Address, "the great task remaining before us."[9]

✈ T I M E L I N E ←

1663	The first documented slave rebellion in the future United States occurs in Gloucester County, Virginia.
1688	Quakers near Philadelphia issue the Germantown Protest, the first documented, public, North American antislavery statement.
1700	Samuel Sewall publishes the antislavery pamphlet *The Selling of Joseph* in Boston.
1712	A slave revolt occurs in New York.
1739	The famous slave rebellion occurs in Stono, South Carolina.
1770	Crispus Attucks is the first black person killed in the cause of American independence at the "Boston Massacre."
1775	What will become the Pennsylvania Abolition Society is organized in Philadelphia.
1776	The Continental Congress agrees to enlist slaves in the Revolutionary Army.
1777	Vermont, not yet a separate state, is the first American territory to ban slavery.
1780	Pennsylvania becomes the first state to abolish slavery—although gradually. Massachusetts is the first to abolish slavery absolutely.
1790	A many-sided conflict begins in French-owned Saint-Domingue, later known as Haiti.

1793	The Fugitive Slave Act permits slave owners or their agents or attorneys to recapture runaway slaves in the free states and territories.
1794	The Mother Bethel African Methodist Episcopal Church is established in Philadelphia, Pennsylvania.
1800	Gabriel Prosser stages an unsuccessful slave insurrection in Henrico County, Virginia.
1808	Congress forbids the further importation of slaves from outside the United States.
1811	A slave revolt occurs in St. John the Baptist Parish, Louisiana.
1816	The American Colonization Society is founded, with the aim of encouraging free blacks to emigrate to Africa.
1820	The Missouri Compromise preserves the balance of power between free and slave states.
1822	Denmark Vesey, a free black man, leads slaves in a revolt in Charleston, South Carolina.
1827	The first issue of *Freedom's Journal*, the nation's first black newspaper, is published.
1829	David Walker publishes "Walker's Appeal in Four Articles," advocating violence as a means to end slavery.
1831	*The Liberator*, William Lloyd Garrison's abolitionist newspaper, begins publication.
1831	Nat Turner leads a rebellion in Virginia.
1833	The American Anti-Slavery Society is created in Philadelphia.

1837	White abolitionist Elijah Lovejoy is killed by a mob in Alton, Illinois.
1838	Black abolitionist Frederick Douglass escapes from slavery to the North.
1839	The ship *Amistad*, under the control of African mutineers, anchors off Long Island.
1841	African mutineers from the *Amistad* are declared free by the U.S. Supreme Court.
1845	*Narrative of the Life of Frederick Douglass* is published.
1849	Harriet Tubman escapes from slavery in Maryland.
1850	The Fugitive Slave Act is amended to enforce the 1793 law, making retrieval of slaves from the northern states and free territories a federal obligation.
1852	Harriet Beecher Stowe's *Uncle Tom's Cabin* is published.
1857	The Supreme Court declares in *Dred Scott v. Sanford* that blacks are not U.S. citizens, and that slaveholders have the right to take slaves into free areas of the country.
1859	John Brown's raid on the federal arsenal and armory in Harpers Ferry, Virginia, fails.
1861	The Civil War begins.
1863	President Lincoln issues the Emancipation Proclamation.
1865	The Civil War ends.
1865	The Thirteenth Amendment to the Constitution abolishes slavery.

❖ Chapter ❖
Notes

Introduction

1. Leslie H. Fishel and Benjamin Quarles, eds., *The Negro American: A Documentary History* (New York: Scott, Foresman, 1967), pp. 28–29.

2. Herbert Aptheker, *American Negro Slave Revolts, 50th Anniversary Edition* (New York: International Publishers, 1993), p. 162.

Chapter 1. Resistance to Slavery Before the Revolution

1. William Lee Miller, *Arguing About Slavery* (New York, Alfred A. Knopf, Inc., 1996), p. 10.

2. National Park Service, "Underground Railroad," *Network to Freedom*, <http://209.10.16.21/TEMPLATE/FrontEnd/learn_a1.cfm> (October 14, 2003).

3. W. Jeffrey Bolster, *Black Jacks: African American Seamen in the Age of Sail* (Cambridge, Mass.: Harvard University Press, 1997), p. 59.

4. Eric Williams, *From Columbus to Castro* (New York: Vintage, 1970), p. 66.

5. Peter Kolchin, *American Slavery 1619–1877* (New York: Hill & Wang, 2003), p. 13.

6. Peter H. Wood, *Black Majority* (New York: W. W. Norton & Company, 1974), p. 320.

7. "Witchcraft in New York: The 1741 Rebellion," *PBS: Africans in America*, <http://www.pbs.org/wgbh/aia/part1/1p286.html> (October 14, 2003).

8. Wood, p. 289.

9. Ibid., p. 306.

10. Samuel Sewall, *The Selling of Joseph* (Boston: Green and Allen, 1700), <http://www.pbs.org/wgbh/aia/part1/1h301t.html> (October 14, 2003).

11. Ibid

12. "The Underground Railroad: Benjamin Lay," *PhillyBurbs.com*, n.d., <http://www.phillyburbs.com/undergroundrailroad/lay.shtml> (October 14, 2003).

13. Leslie H. Fishel and Benjamin Quarles, eds., *The Negro American: A Documentary History* (New York: Scott, Foresman, 1967), pp. 65–66.

CHAPTER 2. SLAVERY AND THE REVOLUTIONARY WAR

1. Michael Lee Lanning, *The African-American Soldier* (Secaucus, N.J.: Carol Publishing, 1997), p. 3.

2. Ibid., p. 16.

3. Leslie H. Fishel and Benjamin Quarles, eds., *The Negro American: A Documentary History* (New York: Scott, Foresman, 1967), p. 40.

4. Sylvia Frey, *Water From the Rock* (N.J.: Princeton University Press, 1991), p. 86.

5. Fishel and Quarles, p. 41.

6. Ibid., p. 42.

7. Marquis de Layfayette, "Lafayette's Testimonial to James Armistead Lafayette," *Skillman & Kirby Libraries – Lafayette College*, n.d., <http://ww2.lafayette.edu/~library/special/specialexhibits/slaveryexhibit/onlineexhibit/testimonial.htm> (September 16, 2003).

8. W. Jeffrey Bolster, *Black Jacks* (Cambridge, Mass.: Harvard University Press, 1997), p. 149.

CHAPTER 3. THE NEW NATION

1. William Lee Miller, *Arguing About Slavery* (New York: Alfred A. Knopf, 1996), p. 80.

2. "Constitution of Pennsylvania—September 28, 1776," *Avalon Project at Yale Law School*, October 14, 2003, <http://www.yale.edu/lawweb/avalon/states/pa08.htm> (October 14, 2003).

3. Richard Newman, Patrick Rael, and Philip Lapsansky, *Pamphlets of Protest* (New York: Routledge, 2001), p. 66.

4. Miller, p. 11.

5. Melvin Drimmer, ed., *Black History: A Reappraisal* (New York: Doubleday & Company, 1968), p. 207.

6. Sylvia Frey, *Water From the Rock* (N.J.: Princeton University Press, 1991), p. 49.

7. Ira Berlin, *Generations of Captivity* (Cambridge, Mass.: Belknap Press, 2003), p. 104.

8. "Address to the Public," *PBS Online*, n.d., <http://www.pbs.org/wgbh/aia/part3/3h252t.html> (September 16, 2003).

9. Berlin, p. 139.

10. Ibid., p. 128.

11. Frey, pp. 96, 228.

12. Ibid., pp. 228–232.

CHAPTER 4. THE ANTISLAVERY MOVEMENT GATHERS FORCE

1. Daniel Coker, "A Dialogue Between a Virginian and an African Minister," reprinted in Richard Newman, Patrick Rael, and Philip Lapsansky, *Pamphlets of Protest* (New York: Routledge, 2001).

2. C. Edward Skeen, *1816: America Rising* (Lexington: University Press of Kentucky, 2003), p. 209.

3. Ibid., p. 210.

4. Ibid.

5. Peter Williams, reprinted in Leslie H. Fishel and Benjamin Quarles, eds., *The Negro American: A Documentary History* (New York: Scott, Foresman, 1967), p. 146.

6. David Walker, reprinted in Fischel and Quarles, p. 151.

7. Newman et al., p. 4.

CHAPTER 5. ABOLITIONISTS ORGANIZE

1. William Lee Miller, *Arguing About Slavery* (New York: Alfred A. Knopf, 1995), p. 67.

2. Ibid., p. 68.

3. Eugene D. Genovese, *Roll Jordan, Roll* (New York: Vintage Books/Random House, 1974), p. 411.

4. Melvin Drimmer, ed., *Black History: A Reappraisal* (New York: Doubleday & Company, 1968), p. 238.

5. Benjamin Quarles, *Black Abolitionists* (New York: Da Capo Press, 1969), p. 23.

6. Miller, p. 85.

7. Henry Mayer, *All On Fire: William Lloyd Garrison and the Abolition of Slavery* (New York: St. Martin's Press, 1998), p. 132.

8. Olive Gilbert (as dictated by Sojurner Truth), "The Narrative of Sojurner Truth: Illegal Sale of Her Son," *A Celebration of Women Writers*, n.d. <http://digital.library. upenn.edu/women/truth/1850/1850-16.html> (September 16, 2003).

9. Miller, p. 206

Chapter 6. The *Amistad* and the New Decade

1. Howard Jones, *Mutiny on the* Amistad (New York: Oxford, 1987), p. 155.

2. William Lee Miller, *Arguing About Slavery* (New York: Alfred A. Knopf, Inc., 1995), p. 402.

3. Frederick Douglass, *Autobiographies: Narrative of the Life, My Bondage and My Freedom, Life and Times* (New York: Literary Classics of the United States, 1994), p. 37.

4. Ibid., pp. 38–39.

5. Frederick Douglass, *Autobiographies: Narrative of the Life, My Bondage and My Freedom, Life and Times*, p. 574.

6. Frederick Douglass, "Narrative of the Life of Frederick Douglass, An American Slave," *Berkeley Digital Library SunSITE*, May 14, 1997, <http://sunsite.berkeley.edu/ Literature/Douglass/Autobiography/04.html> (September 16, 2003).

7. Douglass, *Autobiographies: Narrative of the Life, My Bondage and My Freedom, Life and Times*, p. 588.

8. Ibid., p. 591.

9. William S. McFeely, *Frederick Douglass* (New York: W. W. Norton & Company, 1999), pp. 69–73.

CHAPTER 7. THE REBELS AND THE RUNAWAYS

1. Ira Berlin, *Generations of Captivity* (Cambridge, Mass.: Belknap Press, 2003), p. 15.

2. Ira Berlin, *Many Thousands Gone: The First Two Centuries of Slavery in North America* (Cambridge, Mass.: Belknap Press, 1998), p. 363.

3. Peter Kolchin, *American Slavery 1619–1877* (New York: Hill & Wang, 2003), pp. 156–157.

4. Eugene D. Genovese, *Roll Jordan, Roll* (New York: Vintage Books/Random House, 1974), p. 602.

5. Frederick Douglass, *Autobiographies: Narrative of the Life, My Bondage and My Freedom, Life and Times* (New York: Literary Classics of the United States, 1994), pp. 552–553.

6. Ibid., 24

7. Peter H. Wood, *Black Majority* (New York: W. W. Norton & Company, 1974), pp. 287–288.

8. Kenneth M. Stampp, *The Peculiar Institution: Slavery in the Ante-Bellum South* (New York: Alfred Knopf, 1969), p. 107.

9. Genovese, p. 619.

10. Kolchin, p. 159

11. William Loren Katz, *Breaking the Chains* (New York: Aladdin, 1998), p. 44.

12. William Craft, *Running a Thousand Miles to Freedom; or, the Escape of William and Ellen Craft from Slavery* (London: William Tweedie, 1860), University of North Carolina at Chapel Hill, "Academic Affairs Library," *Documenting the American South* <http://docsouth.dsi.internet2.edu/neh/craft/menu.html> (October 14, 2003).

13. Henry Highland Garnet, "Garnet's 'Call to Rebellion'," *Africans in America*, <http://www.pbs.org/wgbh/aia/part4/4h2937.html> (October 14, 2003).

14. Ibid.

CHAPTER 8. ESCAPE FROM SLAVERY

1. Leslie H. Fishel and Benjamin Quarles, eds., *The Negro American: A Documentary History* (New York: Scott, Foresman, 1967), p. 152.

2. William Still, quoted in Fishel and Quarles, pp. 153–154.

3. William Henry Forman, *The Manhattan*, 1883, <http://jefferson.village.virginia.edu/uncletom/articles/n2ar37at.html> (October 14, 2003).

4. Fischel and Quarles, p. 131.

5. "The Underground Railroad," *PBS: Africans in America*, <http://www.pbs.org/wgbh/aia/part4/4p2944.html> (October 14, 2003).

6. Henry Mayer, *All On Fire: William Lloyd Garrison and the Abolition of Slavery* (New York: St. Martin's Press, 1998), p. 407.

7. Library of Congress, *An American Time Capsule: Three Centuries of Broadsides and Other Printed Ephemera*, <http://memory.loc.gov/ammem/rbpehtml/pehome.html> (October 14, 2003).

8. Benjamin Quarles, *Black Abolitionists* (New York: Da Capo Press, 1969), p. 209.

9. "Anthony Burns Notice," *PBS Online*, n.d., <http://www.pbs.org/wgbh/aia/part4/4h1566.html> (September 16, 2003).

10. Mayer, p. 473.

CHAPTER 9. JOHN BROWN'S RAID

1. Frederick Douglass, *Autobiographies: Narrative of the Life, My Bondage and My Freedom, Life and Times* (New York: Literary Classics of the United States, Inc., 1994), pp. 743–744.

2. William S. McFeely, *Frederick Douglass* (New York: W. W. Norton & Company, 1991), p. 187.

3. Ibid., p. 196.

4. Douglass, p. 759.

5. Stephen B. Oates, *To Purge This Land With Blood* (Amherst: University of Massachusetts Press, 1970), p. 327.

6. Leslie H. Fishel and Benjamin Quarles, eds., *The Negro American: A Documentary History* (New York: Scott, Foresman, 1967), p. 209.

7. Henry Mayer, *All On Fire: William Lloyd Garrison and the Abolition of Slavery* (New York: St. Martin's Press, 1998), p. 505.

8. Abraham Lincoln, "House Divided Speech," ed. Roy P. Baster, *AbrahamLincolnOnline.org*, ©2003, <http://showcase. netins.net/web/creative/lincoln/speeches/house.htm> (October 14, 2003).

CHAPTER 10. ON THE ANTISLAVERY SIDE

1. Louis P. Masur, *1831: Year of Eclipse* (New York: Hill & Wang, 2001), p. 41.

2. Tocqueville, quoted in Masur, p. 41.

3. Ibid., p. 43.

4. Eric Williams, *From Columbus to Castro* (New York: Vintage, 1970), pp. 321–325.

5. William Lee Miller, *Arguing About Slavery* (New York: Alfred A. Knopf, Inc., 1995), p. 502.

6. Leslie H. Fishel and Benjamin Quarles, eds., *The Negro American: A Documentary History* (New York: Scott, Foresman and Company, 1967), p. 212.

7. Miller, p. 495.

8. Ibid.

9. Fishel and Quarles, p. 221.

10. Ibid., p. 216.

11. Michael Lee Lanning, *The African-American Soldier* (Secaucus, N.J.: Carol Publishing, 1997), p. 33.

12. Ibid., p. 34.

13. Fishel and Quarles, p. 224.

14. Frederick Douglass, *Autobiographies: Narrative of the Life, My Bondage and My Freedom, Life and Times* (New York: Literary Classics of the United States, 1994), p. 791.

15. Henry Mayer, *All On Fire: William Lloyd Garrison and the Abolition of Slavery* (New York: St. Martin's Press, 1998), pp. 545–546.

16. Fishel and Quarles, p. 215.

CHAPTER 11. FROM SLAVE TO SOLDIER

1. Leslie H. Fishel and Benjamin Quarles, eds., *The Negro American: A Documentary History* (New York: Scott, Foresman and Company, 1967), p. 217.

2. Michael Lee Lanning, *The African-American Soldier* (Secaucus, N.J.: Carol Publishing, 1997), pp. 44–45.

3. Ibid., pp. 46–47.

4. Ibid., p. 47.

5. Fishel and Quarles, pp. 238–239; Lanning, p. 59.

6. Eric Foner, *A Short History of Reconstruction* (New York: Perennial Library/Harper & Row, 1998), pp. 30–31.

7. Fishel and Quarles, pp. 284–289.

8. Tom Wicker, "If Lincoln Had Not Freed The Slaves," Robert Cowley, ed., *What If 2* (New York: G. M. Putnam Sons, 2001), p. 164.

9. Abraham Lincoln, "The Gettysburg Address," *AbrahamLincolnOnline.org*, ©2003, <http://showcase.netins.net/web/creative/lincoln/speeches/gettysburg.htm> (October 14, 2003).

✧ GLOSSARY ✦

ABOLITION—Ending entirely (especially said of slavery).

BOUNTY—A reward offered for the return of an escaped criminal or slave.

CONDUCTOR—An abolitionist who served as a guide, helping people to travel the Underground Railroad.

EMANCIPATE—To free from bondage.

EXTRADITION—The legal return of a criminal back to the place where the crime was committed to stand trial.

IMMEDIASTS—Those who advocated immediate—rather than gradual—abolition.

INDENTURED SERVANT—A person committed by contract to work as a servant for a specified period of time.

MANUMISSION—The legal process through which a slave owner grants freedom to an individual slave.

RADICAL—Extreme, in ideas or political beliefs.

SECEDE—To legally separate from a state or country to form a new and independent one.

STATIONMASTER—A person who provided a stopover or hiding place on the Underground Railroad.

TEMPERANCE—The moral or political commitment not to drink liquor.

UNDERGROUND RAILROAD—The network of antislavery and abolitionist activists who helped escaped slaves to make their way to freedom in the North or in Canada.

FURTHER READING

Altman, Linda Jacobs. *Slavery and Abolition*. Berkeley Heights, N.J.: Enslow Publishers, Inc., 1999.

Brackett, Virginia. *John Brown: Abolitionist*. Philadelphia: Chelsea House Publishers, 2001.

Butler, Mary G. *Sojourner Truth: From Slave to Activist for Freedom*. New York: PowerPlus Books, 2003.

Clinton, Catherine. *The Black Soldier: 1492 to the Present*. Boston: Houghton Mifflin, 2000.

Douglass, Frederick, *Autobiographies: Narrative of the Life, My Bondage and My Freedom, Life and Times*. New York: Literary Classics of the United States, 1994.

Kromer, Helen. *Amistad: The Slave Uprising Aboard the Spanish Schooner*. Ohio: Pilgrim Press, 1997.

Lanning, Michael Lee. *The African-American Soldier*. Secaucus, N.J.: Carol Publishing, 1997.

McKissack, Fredrick L. and Patricia C. McKissack. *Rebels Against Slavery: American Slave Revolts*. New York: Scholastic, 1996.

Myers, Walter Dean. *Amistad: A Long Road to Freedom*. New York: Dutton Children's Books, 1998.

Yancey, Diane. *Frederick Douglass*. San Diego: Lucent Books, 2003.

Internet Addresses

"Abolition, Anti-Slavery Movements, and the Rise of the Sectional Controversy." *Library of Congress: African American Odyssey.* n.d. <http://lcweb2.loc.gov/ammem/aaohtml/exhibit/aopart3.html>.

"Africans in America." *PBS.* © 1998. <http://www.pbs.org/wgbh/aia/home.html>.

"Learning About the Underground Railroad." *National Park Service.* February 27, 2001. <http://www.cr.nps.gov/ugrr/learn.htm>.

Historic Sites

Boston African American National Historic Site
14 Beacon Street, Suite 503, Boston, MA 02108
(617) 742-5415
boaf@nps.gov
http://www.nps.gov/boaf/index.htm

Frederick Douglass National Historic Site
1411 W Street SE, Washington, D.C. 20020
(202) 426-5961
NACE_Superintendent@nps.gov
http://www.nps.gov/frdo/index.htm

Levi Coffin House
113 U.S. 27 North, P.O. Box 77, Fountain City, IN 47341
(765) 847-2432
http://www.waynet.org/nonprofit/coffin.htm